Growing the Fruit of the Spirit

100 Devotionals for
Farm Families

ENDORSEMENTS

Many who have spent time on a farm recognize the glory of God's creation and plan can be seen everywhere. Truly, farming requires a strong faith. Wisdom is seeing God's hand in the process. Susan Hayhurst and Beth Gormong share some of the wisdom they've witnessed on the farm in *Growing the Fruit of the Spirit: 100 Devotionals for Farm Families*. This book will help you to see God's plan all around you.
—**Dave Blower Jr**., editor, *Indiana Corn & Soybean Post*

Take stock of life's simplicity and the value of family surrounding a working family farm. Beth Gormong and Susan Hayhurst have collected sweet stories from life on the farm that will make readers pause in reflection and appreciation. *Growing the Fruit of the Spirit: 100 Devotionals for Farm Families* gives us an opportunity to understand the challenges of being stewards of our precious resources, the blessing of family, and the necessity of a strong faith.
—**Cindy C. Hoye**, executive director, Indiana State Fair Commission

Refreshing, thought provoking, and an opportunity to harvest new insights from God's word. That is how I describe *Growing the Fruit of the Spirit: 100 Devotionals for Farm Families*. No matter what your day holds, you will find comfort and revelation in each devotion. Written from the heart of farm experience for all of us to reap a harvest of truth and renewed passion.
—**Isabella Chism**, 2nd Vice President Indiana Farm Bureau, and chair, American Farm Bureau Federation Women's Committee

GROWING IN THE SPIRIT | III

Knowing both Susan and Beth, I find their sense of humor and their love for God to be key in the writing of these devotionals. Their ability to weave the day-to-day life of a farm family into teachable moments is refreshing and entertaining as well as engaging the reader to draw closer to God. You'll enjoy reading these devotionals, but you will be blessed as well.
—**Tim Ramseier**, executive director, Wabash Valley Youth for Christ

Reading daily devotionals from Susan Hayhurst and Beth Gormong is like reliving a scene from Forest Gump where Forest says, "My mother says life is like a box of chocolates." Indeed, when you flip open that day's devotional, you never know exactly what you're going to get, but you know it will be sweet and inspiring, wrapped in love, and coated with a kiss of country life that makes it easy to relate. This is one devotional book you will come back to every day.
—**Tom J. Bechman**, editor, *Indiana Prairie Farmer*

Those looking to pair Scripture with the glamorous and not-so-glamorous aspects of farm life will be pleased with Susan Hayhurst and Beth Gormong's book, *Growing the Fruit of the Spirit: 100 Devotionals for Farm Families*. I found myself chuckling at the references to those pesky bee's wings, having dusted plenty of them away myself. I now see that experience in a whole new light.
—**Danica Kirkpatrick**, executive director, Purdue Agricultural Alumni Association

Devotionals help us when we need them most. They are that gentle nudge sometimes that helps us dig deep and reflect on how to continue to grow our own spirituality. Susan and Beth have beautifully related to what we as

agriculturalists live each day and paired them with Bible verses to help fill our cups daily. Readers can't help but feel uplifted and encouraged by their reflections with a book of devotionals that is the perfect way to start or end your day.
—**Alise Nolan**, past president, National Hereford Women

Throughout the Bible, we are led to connect to the land … to the process of planting a seed, nurturing the growth, and ultimately harvesting a product. Susan and Beth connect us to the real experiences of farm life and the inspiration these offer in our faith walk with God. We can relate to the emotions, to the circumstances, to the reactions because we have been there. Each devotion offers inspiring, thoughtful encouragement to lean into the circumstance of life that God provides each day.
—**Beth Archer**, executive director, AgrIInstitute

Farm families are very grounded people. They experience a multitude of challenges through the changing seasons of the year. Walking by faith is a better journey when fueled by the power of God's living word. Beth Gormong and Susan Hayhurst have crafted daily reminders to enlighten your time in your quiet chair as you get ready to face a new day. *Growing the Fruit of the Spirit: 100 Devotionals for Farm Families* will sow seeds of encouragement on your journey.
—**Elaine Froese**, author *of Farming's In-Law Factor: How to Have More Harmony and Less Conflict on Family Farms*. www.elainefroese.com

Do we ever outgrow the need for a bedtime story that captivates our minds and carries us to an imaginary world of joy and peace? *Growing the Fruit of the Spirit: 100 Devotionals for Farm Families: 100 Devotionals for Farm Families* is just that—a bedtime story for adults that uses

God's Word to paint in our minds the love and beauty God has planned for each of us. Kudos To Susan Hayhurst and Beth Gormong for penning devotionals that everyone can relate to, and all will want to read repeatedly.

—**Belinda Puetz**, a Christian wife, mother, and farm advocate

Growing the Fruit of the Spirit: 100 Devotionals for Farm Families speaks to the heart of any person who reads it, because it is written from hearts filled with the love of Jesus Christ. Susan Hayhurst and Beth Gormong are Jesus-loving women who share their life experiences and how God the Father, Son, and Holy Spirit have directed, assisted, and guided them every step of the way. You will walk away feeling lifted and encouraged knowing He provides; all you need to do is pray.

—**DeeDee Sigler**, Christ follower, farm wife, and retired agricultural communication specialist

If you're like most of us, you love a fun story. You also love to reflect on the goodness of God and relate to others' very human moments. In *Growing the Fruit of the Spirit: 100 Devotionals for Farm Families* by Beth Gormong and Susan Hayhurst, you have all three. Entertaining stories of life on the farm. Reflections from God's Word that will help you grow closer to Jesus. And that great feeling you get when you realize, "Yaaaay, I'm not the only one!" I highly recommend this inspiriting book written by two dear and beautiful friends.

—**Jeanette Levellie**, author of *Hello, Beautiful! Finally Love Yourself Just as You Are*, inspirational/humor speaker, and wannabe farmer

Growing the Fruit of the Spirit

100 Devotionals for Farm Families

Beth Gormong & Susan Hayhurst

A Christian Company
ElkLakePublishingInc.com

COPYRIGHT NOTICE

Growing the Fruit of the Spirit: 100 Devotionals for Farm Families

First edition. Copyright © 2023 by Beth Gormong and Susan Hayhurst. The information contained in this book is the intellectual property of Beth Gormong and Susan Hayhurst and is governed by United States and International copyright laws. All rights reserved. No part of this publication, either text or image, may be used for any purpose other than personal use. Therefore, reproduction, modification, storage in a retrieval system, or retransmission, in any form or by any means, electronic, mechanical, or otherwise, for reasons other than personal use, except for brief quotations for reviews or articles and promotions, is strictly prohibited without prior written permission by the publisher.

Scripture taken from THE HOLY BIBLE, NEW INTERNATIONAL VERSION ®. Copyright© 1973, 1978, 1984, 2011 by Biblica, Inc.™. Used by permission of Zondervan

Cover Photograph: Becky Linville
Cover and Interior Design:
Editor(s):Martin Wiles, Deb Haggerty

PUBLISHED BY: Elk Lake Publishing, Inc., 35 Dogwood Drive, Plymouth, MA 02360, 2023

Library Cataloging Data

Names: Gormong, Beth (Beth Gormong) Hayhurst, Susan (Susan Hayhurst)

Growing the Fruit of the Spirit: 100 Devotionals for Farm Families / Beth Gormong and Susan Hayhurst

240 p. 23cm × 15cm (9in × 6 in.)

ISBN-13: 978-1-64949-812-0 (paperback) | 978-1-64949-813-7 (trade hardcover) | 978-1-64949-814-4 (trade paperback) | 978-1-64949-815-1 (e-book)

Key Words: farm family devotional; Christian farm devotional; farm wife devotional; farm wife book; farm gift book devotional; daily devotional; encouraging Christian devotional

Library of Congress Control Number: 2023932692 Nonfiction

DEDICATION

FROM BETH ...

To Jeff, who encouraged me to write when I wanted to watch television, who read and approved my stories even when they involved him, and without whom I'd have no book to write. What a crazy, beautiful life we've created together. I love you ... more.

To my father-in-law, Larry Gormong. Thank you for opening your arms wide to this city girl.

To my Gormong family: L, R, J, J, J, J, J, R, R, R, J, K, J, J, J, and J. Thank you for sharing your stories and lives with me even though my name starts with a "B." I love you all.

In loving memory of my mother-in-law, Rita Gormong, my farm-life mentor, confidant, and second mom. You are so missed.

FROM SUSAN ...

To Terry, my honeybear and farmer, who cheered me on at the first mention of this book idea with Beth. I wouldn't be writing about farm life if not for the Lord and you. I love you so much.

To Lillian and Hayley, my dear daughters. Living your farm adventures with you has brought me crazy laughter, joy, blessings, and so much more to write about. Many snurffles.

Thank you, Jesus, for my writing passion and the Holy Spirit empowering me through this project. To God be the glory!

TABLE OF CONTENTS

Endorsements ii
Dedication ix
Table of Contents ix
Acknowledgments xv

LOVE

1. Loving a Farmer—Susan 1
2. Old Red Goes Home—Beth 3
3. Unconditional Love—Susan 5
4. Evenings on the Back Deck—Beth 7
5. Gaining a German Daughter—Susan 9
6. Pickup Basketball—Beth 11
7. A Ministry of Presence—Susan 13
8. Cocker Spaniel Farm Dog—Beth 15
9. Creative Dating—Susan 17
10. A Farm Style Valentine's Date—Beth 19
11. God with Us—Susan 21

JOY

12. Dumpster Cheering—Susan 25
13. Will We Have Thanksgiving This Year—Beth 27
14. Celebrate Everything—Susan 29
15. Farm Sledding—Beth 31
16. Presidential Herefords—Susan 33
17. The Love of Farming Never Dies—Beth 35

18. Sunshine Hour—Susan 37
19. Farm Meals with Rita—Beth 39
20. Desire Is by Design—Susan 41
21. Bad Boy Buggy—Beth 43
22. Green Acres, Hoosier Style—Susan 45

PEACE

23. Early Morning/Late Night—Beth 49
24. Fertilize Your Mind—Susan 51
25. There's a Tick on My Back—Beth 53
26. Bloom Where You Are Planted—Susan 55
27. The Case of the Missing Doorknob—Beth 57
28. Act of Obedience—Susan 59
29. Resting by the Road—Beth 61
30. The Cross Terry Built—Susan 63
31. Eagles Overhead—Beth 65
32. Ministry to Farm—Beth 67

PATIENCE

33. Rain, Go Away, Rain, Come Back—Beth 71
34. The Daddy Months—Susan 73
35. Tractor Napping—Beth 75
36. Your Prayer Closet—Susan 77
37. Watch the Road—Beth 79
38. Keeping a Sense of Humor—Susan 81
39. The Case of the Mouse in the Oil Bottle—Beth 83
40. Moving Antiques in a Livestock Trailer—Susan 85
41. You're Due in May—Beth 87
42. What's a Planned Vacation—Susan 89
43. Experienced Driver—Beth 91

KINDNESS

44. Cornered by a Bull—Beth 95
45. Prodigal Annie—Susan 97
46. Locked in the Cage—Beth 99
47. Help! My Child Is Joining 4-H—Susan 101
48. Saving Stray Cats—Beth 103

49. German Hospitality—Susan 105
50. Freezing Corn—Beth 107
51. Earthly Angels—Susan.. 109
52. The Drive-By Mother-in-Law—Beth 111
53. Wedding at the Farm—Susan 113
54. Green Thumb, Brown Thumb—Beth 115

Goodness

55. God's Timing is Perfect—Susan 119
56. First-Time Tractor Driver—Beth 121
57. Unexpected Groceries—Susan 123
58. Ah, the Smell of Money—Beth 125
59. Heed the Nudging—Susan 127
60. The Anhydrous Thief—Beth 129
61. Watch What You Pray For—Susan 131
62. A Texas Olive Grove—Beth 133
63. Never Say Never—Susan 135
64. A Stinky Situation—Beth 137

Faithfulness

65. Begotten Herefords—Susan 141
66. What Does a Farmer Do—Beth............................. 143
67. Rooted in Farming—Susan................................... 145
68. Faulty Equipment—Beth 147
69. Flickering Lights—Susan...................................... 149
70. Vegas—Beth 151
71. Called to Pray—Susan.. 153
72. City Girl Moves to the Farm—Beth....................... 155
73. Do Not Worry—Susan 157
74. Leaving the Farm—Beth 159
75. Great Is Your Faithfulness—Susan 161

Gentleness

76. My Chicken Has a Bone in It—Beth 165
77. Even Cows Like Music—Susan 167
78. A Strong Old House—Beth................................... 169
79. Tools of the Trade—Susan 171

80. Sweeping the Bin—Beth 173
81. Chickens and a Dog Named Sam—Susan 175
82. Farming Is Not Gardening—Beth 177
83. An Unusual Cousin Reunion—Susan 179
84. Long Distance Cow Herding—Beth 181
85. Mentoring a Rookie—Susan 183

SELF-CONTROL

86. A Rat and White Tennis Shoes—Susan 187
87. Sunday Morning Chores—Beth 189
88. A Short Cut to a Farm Show—Susan........................191
89. Bees Wings—Beth 193
90. A Bull Meets a Rock—Susan 195
91. Down in a Ditch—Beth 197
92. Master Farmer—Susan 199
93. Auger Miracle—Beth 201
94. Pursuing God-given Passions—Susan 204
95. Town Day—Beth 205
96. Cow Sightings—Susan 207
97. The Secret Mission—Beth 209
98. First Fruits—Susan 211
99. Hawk at the Birdfeeder—Beth 213
100. A Lesson from a Woodpecker—Susan 215
About the Authors 217

ACKNOWLEDGMENTS

From Beth

Susan, cousin by marriage, friend by heart. Thank you for taking a chance on this book with me. I love you, my praying, farming, and writing soul-sister.

Barb Howe, I've always wanted to be like you. Thank you for all the editing work you put into making my words sound pretty.

From Susan

Beth, it's been a joy to collaborate with you on this book. Who knew us two city girls would be writing about farm life? God did. Love you so much.

DeeDee Sigler, thank you for your excellent editing skills and non-stop encouraging words through this volume's process. You were the Lord's instrument in matchmaking my farmer, Terry, with me. You are a priceless treasure and friend of the heart.

Indiana Prairie Farmer magazine staff, thank you for your permission to use some of my "Hayhurst's Hayloft" columns in this book's devotionals.

From Both

Susan and I are especially grateful to Elk Lake Publishing, Inc. and the entire Elk Lake family: Deb

Haggerty, our publisher; Derinda Babcock, our book cover designer; and Martin Wiles, our editor. Thank you for all the work you did for us and do for the kingdom of God. You deserve many diamonds in your heavenly crowns.

The earth is the Lord's, and everything in it,
the world, and all who live in it.—Psalm 24:1

LOVE

But the fruit of the Spirit is love, joy, peace, forbearance, kindness, goodness, faithfulness, gentleness and self-control. Against such things there is no law.

—Galatians 5:22–23

1. LOVING A FARMER

> Love is patient, love is kind. It does not envy, it does not boast, it is not proud. It does not dishonor others; it is not self-seeking.
>
> (1 Corinthians 13:4–5)

Several years ago, my husband Terry offered to respond to my *Indiana Prairie Farmer* Valentine's Day column I wrote about how I love him. The column was my rendition of poet Elizabeth Barrett Browning's *Sonnet 43*, "How Do I Love Thee? Let Me Count the Ways." Here is Terry's version.

> How do I know my farm wife loves me? Her love is patient when at night, I have the faint smell of manure.
> Her love is kind when date night is postponed, again.
> Her love does not envy when vacation is canceled.
> Her love hopes for more time when I fall asleep during our two-way conversation.
> Her love is not self-seeking when we go to the National Farm Machinery Show on her Valentine's birthday.
> Her love is not childlike when we drive through implement dealerships instead of car dealerships.
> Her love trusts when I ask her to take hog manure samples.
> Her love perseveres when she helps load hogs into the semi-trailer.
> Her love keeps no record of wrong when she gets shocked by the electric fence.

> Her love allows her to put away any offensive thoughts when she's holding the cow's tail during artificial insemination.
> Her love is not easily angered when she recovers the tools I borrowed.
> And now these three remain: the faith of my farm wife and the hope and love of my farm wife, but the greatest of these is the love of our Lord.

While it's not necessary to count the ways we love our spouses or family members, loving them as Jesus teaches us is a good reminder to pause and pray for the innumerable ways they bless us. Does their faith encourage yours? Do you worship or pray together? Are daily devotions shared? Do they invite you to ride with them in the equipment (smile)?

God, you not only knit us individually in our mother's womb, but you also brought us together as husband and wife. Thank you for the wonderful privilege of your love, which sets the best example for us being joined together. Amen.

Take your journal and write the ways your spouse blesses you. Then bless them in return.

—Susan

2. OLD RED GOES HOME

> If I go up to the heavens, you are there; if I make my bed in the depths, you are there. If I rise on the wings of the dawn, if I settle on the far side of the sea, even there your hand will guide me, your right hand will hold me fast.
> (Psalm 139:8—10)

Visiting Grandpa Johnson meant riding in the bed of his prized '66 Chevy pickup, Old Red. We bounced across the farm—over hills and bumpy fields—or rode to town for orange sherbet push-ups.

After Grandpa died, Old Red was passed down to my cousin, Billy, and then to my brother, Ron, who lovingly repaired the engine, restored the paint-peeling exterior to the original red color, and updated the interior with a newer front row seat that had seatbelts. Old Red became his architectural firm's work truck and constant companion to all worksites.

One day Ron gave me a call. "We're retiring. It's time for Old Red to go home to an Indiana farm. You want him?"

Did I want Old Red? Oh my, yes! If I could have done flips, I would have. I pictured myself driving down country roads—the wind whipping my hair, elbow hanging out the window—while I hauled home tomato plants and mulch.

Old Red came to our farm until Jeff and I decided to retire from farming. We began the process of moving to the city. But what would happen to our beloved Johnson family truck? Old Red belonged on a farm, not in the middle of a city.

God had a perfect plan for the next step of Old Red's journey. My cousin, Carl, leaped at the chance to be the truck's next caregiver. Now Old Red lives at a landscape nursery just a few miles from the farm where our grandparents lived and minutes from the cemetery where they are buried. Old Red is back where he belongs.

Sometimes God's path leads us on a life journey far away from where we started. And sometimes, he brings us right back home again. But even though we don't see our life's entire map from the beginning, God provides family and friends to love, nurture, and join us on our travels.

Lord, thank you for providing, protecting, and being present through every twist and turn we encounter.

Can you thank God for the unexpected roads he has led you down?

—Beth

3. UNCONDITIONAL LOVE

A new command I give you: Love one another. As I have loved you, so you must love one another.

(John 13:34)

An invitation to a wedding heralds a new beginning, a new commitment, and the promise of unending love. When our daughter, Lillian, was planning her wedding ceremony, she asked her paternal grandma, Betty Jo, to share Scripture. Betty Jo was thrilled and included personal testimony of her and her husband Dale's foundations of marriage.

"God has given us many invitations in his Word," said Betty Jo. "One is Revelation 19:9. 'Blessed are those who are invited to the wedding supper of the Lamb.' Why did God give us this invitation? John 3:16 tells us, 'For God so loved the world that he gave his one and only Son, that whoever believes in him shall not perish but have eternal life.' This Scripture shows God's unconditional love."

She also shared God's definition of love from 1 Corinthians 13:4–5: "Love is patient, love is kind. It does not envy, it does not boast, it is not proud. It does not dishonor others, it is not self-seeking, it is not easily angered, it keeps no record of wrongs." If you love someone you will be loyal to him no matter the cost.

Betty Jo emphasized that she and Dale built their lives and marriage on the foundation of God's Word. "Our love and obedience to God kept him in the center of our marriage. This is our hope and prayer for both of you."

Their marriage lasted fifty-six years and set an example for children, grandchildren, and great-grandchildren.

Lillian and her husband's wedding invitation intentionally proclaimed their love for God, farming, and her husband's daughter, Kaelynn. The Lord's unconditional love was the centerpiece.

Jesus Christ's invitation to accept him as your Lord and Savior awaits your reply.

What does God's unlimited love mean to you?

—Susan

4. EVENINGS ON THE BACK DECK

> And let us consider how we may spur one another on toward love and good deeds, not giving up meeting together, as some are in the habit of doing, but encouraging one another—and all the more as you see the Day approaching.
>
> (Hebrews 10:24–25)

Summer means lengthening sunsets, fireflies, and blooming flowers. When the girls were small, summer on our farm also involved evenings sitting together on my in-laws' back deck, watching the girls play in a tiny blowup pool. The pool time was more about staying cool and playing with toys than swimming. Their tanned legs pretzeled together to fit the three of them in the pool.

Those summertime evenings meant popsicles on the deck, watching the sunset as three generations enjoyed the cool breeze after a long day of work. Many evenings, we shared a simple supper of sandwiches, chips, and a can of cold pop in comfortable silence—peppered with moments of high-pitched giggling or dogs barking at passing trucks.

Sounds so romantic, eh? Not at all. Not all the time anyway. There were aching muscles, stinky hogs, flies, mosquitoes, and arguments over what would be done the next day. Added to this were crying, overtired girls—disappointed to have to head home for a bath. As I look back through the lens of time, I realize family living life together was a blessing.

Seeing beauty can be difficult in the middle of the messiness of life. When we're exhausted and just want to eat supper and get to bed, spending a few moments with the grandparents might be low on the priorities list. When we've been working together all day, getting away from each other feels really good. But in reality, togetherness creates the best memories.

Lord, thank you for our family in all its messiness. Thank you for ordinary, mundane days that are formed from the simple minutes of our lives yet leave us with sweet memories.

Ask God to help you see the ordinary of today through the perspective of time.

—Beth

5. GAINING A GERMAN DAUGHTER

> And I pray that you, being rooted and established in love, may have power, together with all the Lord's holy people, to grasp how wide and long and high and deep is the love of Christ.
>
> (Ephesians 3:17–18)

Taking three years of German and being active in the German club in high school were both highlights for me. Added to that fun, family and friends hosted a teenage German exchange student, Toby, who captured the heart of our school.

Our daughter Hayley, who was taking German in high school, said she wanted to host a German girl during her senior year. Hayley, my husband Terry, our older daughter Lillian, and I jumped at the opportunity. We chose Lisa from eastern Germany.

I wondered if she would fit in with our family and life on the farm. I had prayed that the Lord would lead us to the right student. Boy, did he ever!

Lisa's conversational English was excellent, she was very flexible, she professed to be an evangelical Christian, and she lived next door to her maternal grandparents, who raised Katahdin sheep. Lisa loved helping her grandpa Opa feed and take care of the sheep daily. She also planned to be a veterinarian.

Lisa was introduced to our busy life the minute she landed in Indianapolis. We explained we weren't headed home but to the Indiana State Fair Celebration of Champions. Lisa embraced the experience fully.

When we returned to the farm, Lisa slid right into American life. She happily fed cattle and helped make meals during harvest while keeping a 4.0 GPA, actively participating in the church youth group, and serving as unofficial "social coordinator" for other school exchange students.

How could we have doubted? Just as the Lord loved and grafted us as branches into his vine, he answered our prayers exponentially with our love for Lisa, our forever third daughter.

Precious Father, we count it such a blessing that we are all a part of your family.

How have you stepped out of your comfort zone? Trust the Lord and take a leap of faith today.

—Susan

6. PICKUP BASKETBALL

I know that there is nothing better for people than to be happy and to do good while they live. That each of them may eat and drink, and find satisfaction in all their toil—this is the gift of God.

(Ecclesiastes 3:12–13)

"Can we play basketball, please?" fourteen-year-old Jeff and ten-year-old Joe begged their dad. Their ultimate daily goal was to finish the chores quickly so they could challenge their college-aged uncle, Ron, to a game.

"Finish the chores, and we'll see," Larry said, handing them feed buckets.

The boys ran off to feed the pigs, willing to do any chore assigned without complaint if finishing the job meant playing ball at the end of the day.

Soon they were on the court, playing two on two—Larry and Joe against Ron and Jeff. This was Hoosier basketball at its finest. The goal was nailed to the side of a gray metal granary. Their uniforms were dirty, sweaty, bib overalls and work boots that crunched on cinder chips.

Uncle Ron always seemed to eke out a win. In reality, he'd let the young boys get close enough to feel the hope of winning, then pull ahead at the last minute.

Grandpa watched from the sideline until one of the players threw him the ball, urging him to take a few shots. But Grandma watched from inside the house in case Grandpa got too involved in the game. Then she'd stick her head out the door and order him to come inside because she worried about his weak heart.

Basketball games after chores were a highlight of farm life. A fun game with family made the work of the day more enjoyable.

God wants us to work hard and do good with our life. He also wants us to enjoy our days, our family, and our friends.

Lord, give us the strength to work hard, yet remind us to leave time for enjoyment.

Do you only see the burden of our "toiling the earth?" Where can you create time for relaxation and fun with your family?

—Beth

7. A MINISTRY OF PRESENCE

> Brothers and sisters, choose seven men from among you who are known to be full of the Spirit and wisdom. We will turn this responsibility over to them and will give our attention to prayer and the ministry of the word.
> (Acts 6:3–4)

Have you heard of servant leadership? Servant leaders aim to serve the people who surround them. Such leaders are not concerned with gaining power but sharing responsibility with grace and dignity.

My late father-in-law, Dale, was a servant leader and highly respected in his community. He was committed to God. Nothing was more important to him than living for Jesus Christ, reading and studying the Word, and worshiping his Lord. His daily walk with Jesus was evident, whether he was tilling ground on the family farm or sharing his financial wisdom with clients at the family's accounting office in town.

Although his vocational calling was to follow his parents in their accounting business, Dale's passions focused on their farm, Polled Hereford cattle, and the Lord. My mother-in-law, Betty Jo, said they seldom took a vacation because Dale's relaxation was walking among the cows.

He was a quiet, soft-spoken man with a dry wit. Community service was ingrained in him by his father,

Kendall. Dale followed his dad's legacy in many volunteer financial leadership positions, where they collectively served humbly for over one hundred years.

When the church doors were open, Dale was there. He either sang, led a Sunday school class, or gave the treasurer's report at a local or district board meeting. For more than fifty years, he also participated weekly in the extended family's local radio station's program for shut-ins.

When Dale died, his presence in the community and his love for the Lord were evidenced by the outpouring of people and their sharing of treasured memories. A former pastor's wife, who knew my in-laws well, shared how Dale and Betty Jo's marriage commitment was a "ministry of presence."

Whom do you know who has such a presence because their hearts are focused on servant leadership like Jesus?

Lord, you are the one who set a precedent as our servant leader. Help us to model your example.

Ask the Lord to manifest a servant leader's heart in you.

—Susan

8. COCKER SPANIEL FARM DOG

Take delight in the Lord, and he will give you the desires of your heart.

(Psalms 37:4)

When Jeff and I moved from Detroit to the farm, we brought Sassy, our purebred cocker spaniel dog. She had been born and raised in the city and regularly visited the local dog groomers for trims and pampering. She was a city dog through and through, with her long blond hair and a fancy bandanna tied around her neck.

But soon after we moved to the country, Sassy began going with Jeff to the farm. One day, she decided she didn't want to come home. Sassy moved out of our house and made herself at home on the farm. She ran around the barn lot as if she didn't have fancy breeding and high-maintenance fur.

Sassy loved nothing more than to roll in the grass and jump on an ATV with the guys. Soon, Sassy's fur became matted. She didn't care one bit that we used scissors to cut the knots out. She could care less that she smelled like a farm and not perfumed shampoo. She was too busy living life to worry about her appearance.

I relate to Sassy's feelings about her adopted home.

I didn't grow up on a farm. I had no idea what farm life meant. And I will admit I didn't and still don't like smelling like a pig or cleaning mud off my Sunday shoes. But I do love the smell of freshly plowed dirt, the sound of cows mooing in the distance, and the sight of soybeans poking through the soil. Morning walks down country roads are one of my favorite moments. Sassy and I discovered the farm was the perfect home for us city girls.

Lord, thank you for a farm to call home. Never let us take simple blessings for granted.

What do you love about living on a farm?

—Beth

9. CREATIVE DATING

> From him the whole body, joined and held together by every supporting ligament, grows and builds itself up in love, as each part does its work.
>
> (Ephesians 4:16)

I confess that I'm a romantic. I always imagined my husband would drive a sporty two-seater, dine with me at elegant restaurants, and take me to exotic destinations. Little did I know I would marry a farmer who drives a combine with a buddy seat, considers a drive-through to be eating out, and invites me to the Farm Progress Show.

Farmers' schedules often involve long hours, haphazard delays, and inclement weather. Planned excursions and specialty restaurants are placed on the back burner when they need parts, move equipment between fields, or get emergency calls from aging parents.

What is a couple to do? Plan creative dating activities!

While my sweet mother-in-law, Betty Jo, said there was no such thing as "dating your spouse" when she and my late father-in-law Dale were married, she understands the need to spend time together. She encouraged dates that revolved around the farm. Seize the moment when your spouse asks you to go with them on a parts run. Doing so might net you a Dairy Queen Blizzard. Agree with that drive through of the implement dealership. While your spouse may drool a bit over the expensive machinery, you're showing them you are interested in what they do.

Riding sidesaddle in the combine or tractor while discussing farm goals brings purpose and joy. Stuffing your young children in the cab with you and your spouse while working ground is even more fun if a picnic basket with delicious treats is involved. Getaways involving livestock sales and agricultural conferences can include nice places to stay, new restaurants to enjoy, and lots of laughter with each other and friends, making cheerful memories.

Ephesians 4 points out that we bolster our marriage ligament by ligament when we compromise and build each other up as we cherish time together.

Father God, help me seize the daily moments to spend one-on-one time with my spouse and family.

Honor and surprise your spouse with a special date.

—Susan

10. A FARM STYLE VALENTINE'S DATE

Whoever would foster love covers over an offense, but whoever repeats the matter separates close friends.
(Proverbs 17:9)

"We need to make one stop before we go to the restaurant." Jeff handed me a broken tractor belt as he sat in the driver's seat.

"Okay, no problem." I sat the part on the car floor and grabbed a leftover fast-food napkin from the glove box, carefully cleaning the grease off my hands before I touched my lovely Valentine's Day dress.

An hour later, I was no longer okay. I was starving and fed up with all the stops trying to find the correct replacement part. I watched the sun move lower in the sky until nearly bedtime for our girls. No time for dinner and a movie. Our romantic evening out without the kids was ruined. I was angry. Jeff was frustrated.

We found a restaurant that didn't need reservations and ate without speaking, mulling over our irritations. We left the restaurant and headed straight home.

Well, that was a disaster. I fled the cold silence of the car for the warmth of the house, where my little daughters' arms begged for hugs and kisses. Soon the affection from our daughters worked to soften both our hearts until we were able to reconcile our petty annoyances.

Have you ever felt the disappointment of a date or entire day gone wrong? Perhaps miscommunication created conflict, too much anticipation led to unmet expectations, or unexpected obstacles destroyed well-intended plans.

The book of wisdom, Proverbs, reminds us to love even when disappointed—when spouses, family, friends, or work associates let us down. We are to foster love amid offense.

Lord, help us whisper when we feel like yelling, hug instead of running away, and forgive when we want to charge forward and fight. May we foster love in every offense.

To whom do you need to reconcile? Start now.

—Beth

11. GOD WITH US

> When they [shepherds] had seen him, they spread the word concerning what had been told them about this child, and all who heard it were amazed at what the shepherds said to them. But Mary treasured up all these things and pondered them in her heart.
>
> (Luke 2:17–19)

Close your eyes and imagine Mary. She was a teenager who gave birth to a baby in a stable, knowing he was the world's Savior. Was she scared, intimidated, shocked? Was she missing the comforts of her home—warmth, food, family? Did she wonder if Joseph would be a good father?

Scripture tells us Mary cherished the lowly shepherds who heralded her son Jesus's birth. She surely listened awestruck as angels glorified the new King. Later, Mary humbly watched as the Magi came to worship the child at the house where she and Joseph lived. She understood the reaction of all who heard the news and was full of joy because her baby was Immanuel, God with us.

Mary must have contemplated the disgrace she might suffer, like being disgraced for having a child out of wedlock. Yet God had called her to bear his Son who would forgive people for their sins.

Pondering all Mary experienced, let alone treasuring it, is a challenge. What do you cherish? Perhaps your treasures are outstanding harvest yields, full bins, and new equipment. A healthy family and a comfortable home may rank at the top of your priority list.

Our hearts hold what we store in them. 1 Samuel 16:7 says, "The Lord does not look at the things people look at. People look at the outward appearance, but the LORD looks at the heart." If we ponder the joys and blessings the Lord gives us, our hearts will overflow, just as Mary's did so long ago.

Thank you, God, that you are always with us. Help us to examine our hearts with your treasure of salvation in mind.

What is in your heart today? List five blessings and five concerns. Thank the Lord for the blessings and give the concerns to him in prayer.

—Susan

JOY

But the fruit of the Spirit is love, joy, peace, forbearance, kindness, goodness, faithfulness, gentleness and self-control. Against such things there is no law.

—Galatians 5:22–23

12. DUMPSTER CHEERING

The one who has clean hands and a pure heart, who does not trust in an idol or swear by a false god. They will receive blessing from the Lord and vindication from God their Savior.

(Psalm 24:4–5)

Hosting special events at the farm frequently necessitates a honey-do list. While my husband, Terry, says he keeps his working lists in his head, I prefer a clean sheet of paper and an attention-getting black Sharpie to check off the accomplishments.

At the top of my—not Terry's—to-do list is renting a dumpster. What that refuse bin symbolizes makes it so purposeful. A dumpster is for clearing and hauling away junk.

A farmer's junk—scrap recyclables, odds and ends, old equipment, and trucks—is considered treasure and usually stowed on the back forty. I asked my husband why these things were hidden from public view if they were so important. His response, "I don't want people taking my valuables!"

Trash hauling has been celebrated several times at Hayhurst Farms, all to make ourselves presentable. We have welcomed international farmers, numerous state and national legislators' forums, and community and state agricultural events. The most cleansing dumpster rental held lots of unsightly "treasures" to make way for hosting our daughter's wedding.

Sometimes I need a dumpster to off-load the worries, concerns, idols, and frustrations that dog my mind and heart. I certainly don't want to display them in brilliant colors. The good news is all I need is to seek the Lord, the forgiver of all the refuse hidden or buried in our hearts. Psalm 103:11–12 says, "For as high as the heavens are above the earth, so great is his love for those who fear him; as far as the east is from the west, so far he has removed our transgressions from us." That is something to cheer about.

Father God, what spiritual or physical clutter do I need to toss out today? Help me to follow your Holy Spirit's nudging that I might have a clean heart. Thank you.

Have you been holding too much inside for too long? Now is the time for renewal.

—Susan

13. WILL WE HAVE THANKSGIVING THIS YEAR?

> May the peoples praise you, God; may all the peoples praise you. The land yields its harvest; God, our God, blesses us.
>
> (Psalm 67:5–6)

Every farm family knows the drama around the fall and winter holidays. Harvest season begins with excitement and energy, but weariness and anxiety take over somewhere around mid-November. By Thanksgiving, everyone is on edge. Will we get to visit family for Thanksgiving? Will the harvesting be done? Will the weather hold out until we're done or dry out enough for us to get back in and finish? Fall is the best and worst of seasons.

That's especially true for us city wives. We didn't read the fine print on the marriage certificate, stating holidays might be canceled due to rain. I remember being so devastated the first Thanksgiving I went to my parent's house without Jeff. I thought for sure they would be upset with him and believe he wasn't a good husband. I should have known better. Both my parents grew up on farms. They understood weather determines the work schedule.

Over the years, I've realized a simple farming fact: our lives are at the mercy of the weather and broken machinery. But let's not forget that other cause of joy.

Every holiday spent with family is extra memorable—just as the last day of the planting and harvesting season is cause for celebration. I'm thankful for the blessing of working with the land, especially when the weather cooperates. And I'm grateful for the family who eagerly waits to celebrate with us.

Lord, thank you for the holidays, but more importantly, thank you for our family who loves us even when we can't gather.

Are you able to be grateful for harvests that cut into holiday gatherings?

—Beth

14. CELEBRATE EVERYTHING

> Rejoice in the Lord always, I will say it again: Rejoice!
> (Philippians 4:4)

I was raised in a home where my ever-hospitable mom welcomed family, friends, neighbors, and homesick college students to our dining table. She was adept at hosting celebrations for any occasion.

When I married my husband, Terry, putting out a similar welcome mat was important to me. A vivid yellow ceramic plaque in my kitchen proclaims, "Until further notice ... celebrate everything!" That sums up my philosophy.

We've entertained farm visitors for tours and cookouts and invited local college students to conduct research, soil samplings, and their drone capabilities. Terry and I tearfully hugged each other when trusses for our new machinery shed arrived following a terrible fire. The shed has housed multiple significant birthday and anniversary parties. The farm hosted our oldest daughter's wedding and was the site of her first baby's gender reveal event, featuring pink smoke billowing from the four-wheel drive tractor's exhaust.

Our two daughters, Lillian and Hayley, have fond memories of coming home from school with good news, knowing I would play Beach Boys music and dance around the kitchen. Good report cards and school recognition, new jobs, 4-H achievements, getting baptized, and awesome harvest yields were all causes of festivity. Sporting crazy, oversized sunglasses and costume hats brought giggles and eye-rolling when the girls stepped off the school bus. Even sibling rivalry was met with pool noodles jousting.

The girls and I waited with bated breath and tuned ears for equipment pulling in the driveway to signify harvest completion. Running out to the barn lot to hug Terry, we linked arms for a do-si-do. Terry's dinner was served on the ruby red plate of honor, emblazoned with "You are special today."

John 20 highlights Jesus revealing himself to Mary Magdalene by the tomb. She was overjoyed to see him and cried out, "Rabboni!" Then, telling the good news to the disciples, she said, "I have seen the Lord!" What rejoicing must have filled her heart.

Lord of celebration, give us eyes to see and hearts to express joy wherever you direct us.

An unexpected celebration is a gift from God. Plan one today.

—Susan

15. FARM SLEDDING

A cheerful heart is good medicine.

(Proverbs 17:22)

Who needs a hill to sled? Why pack up the kids and drive them to the community park or some predetermined perfect neighborhood hill when the snow comes?

Farm kids know how to make their own fun. Sledding on our farm meant finding a grain bin lid attached with a chain to the tractor. Farm sledding is like water tubing, only in the winter. And instead of swimsuits and sunscreen, the proper attire includes Carhartt Overalls, insulated gloves, and work boots.

The best part of farm sledding is that the cousins could all pile on the huge "sled" together and head off, laughing and squealing through the snow-covered fields. The goal was to be the last one to fly off the sled. The ride was as much fun for the tractor driver as for the sled riders.

This type of sledding was perfect for me, too. I stood inside my cozy, warm house with my mother-in-law and sisters-in-law and watched the jocularity through the living room window. Pappy, dads, and uncles dealt with the cold weather and wrangled runaway marshmallow-shaped toddlers. My job was to get Rita's hot chocolate into steaming mugs, ready to warm up cold hands and empty bellies.

How wonderful that farm life revolves around the family's schedule. What a blessing that we can stop working in the middle of a school-canceled snow day to spend time having fun with children, grandchildren, nieces, and nephews. I think God is pleased when we give our family high priority.

Lord, thank you for the spontaneous family time that living on a farm allows. May we never take that privilege for granted.

Spend a few minutes having fun as a family today.

—Beth

16. PRESIDENTIAL HEREFORDS

> I have no need of a bull from your stall or of goats from your pens, for every animal of the forest is mine, and the cattle on a thousand hills.
>
> (Psalm 50:9–10)

In my husband Terry's life, no business or leisure trip is complete without seeing Hereford cattle. During a visit to San Antonio, Texas, my brother Bob, and his wife Jolanda, offered to take Terry and me on a day-long excursion, including the Lyndon B. Johnson National Historical Park in Texas hill country.

As we drove through the expansive 1,500-acre park, Terry's eyes were focused acutely on cattle sightings. Suddenly, Terry spied a large group of Herefords about a half mile down the road.

"Bob, you can't just drive by those cattle," I warned. "Find a place to pull off and park. We could be here awhile."

Bob had barely pulled off next to a fence and put the car in park when Terry jumped from the front passenger seat and stepped up to the fence.

"Sook, cow, sook! Sook, cow, sook!"

A chorus of moos answered him. Soon, many cows from fencerows and behind low hills came our way.

What a sight. Man and beasts delighted in the attention.

Terry's blue eyes lit up like stadium lights as Herefords from the late president's lineage spoke to him. I cried joyfully as I watched my husband have the time of his life. I pulled out my phone, recorded thirty seconds of the exchange, and sent the video to our girls—Hayley in London, England, and Lillian in Indiana. They were thrilled for their dad.

When I married Terry, his love for Herefords rubbed off on me. I came to love the dark red and white cattle. The Lord has shown me never to pass up an opportunity to enjoy them with my spouse. Watching for Herefords on every trip is worth it.

Creator of all things, thank you for showing me how to embrace my husband's joy.

Give God praise for the many things in your life where he gives you great gladness.

—Susan

17. THE LOVE OF FARMING NEVER DIES

> The Lord God took the man and put him in the Garden of Eden to work it and take care of it.
>
> (Genesis 2:15)

My dad, a little boy with coal black hair and mischievous eyes, grew up working the hilly fields of southern Indiana with his dad and younger brother. As a young man, Dad was hired to run a turkey farm and thought his life's path was determined. The owner trusted him with a house and a truck and left Dad in charge of the operation.

But God had other plans and called Dad to be a pastor. Yet, the love of the land never left him. He planted huge gardens everywhere he lived, harvesting the produce for my mom to can and freeze each fall. At ninety-five, he was still out growing tomatoes in his small garden—some plants for him and some for his neighbor. And at every visit to our farm, he climbed onto the machinery and marveled at the advanced technology of autosteer.

Dad's not alone in his appreciation of farming. I've watched my father-in-law bend over to test the soil, the dirt slipping through his fingers. My husband, too, lights up talking about the crop yield and weather forecasts.

Farming and the love of the land take deep roots in a person's soul. I'm not surprised that the first location mentioned in the Bible is the garden of Eden or that the first job entailed tending the land.

Farming may be a stressful and exhausting career, but working in agriculture is also a richly satisfying and soul-nourishing occupation.

Lord, thank you for giving us the responsibility of caring for your creation and feeding humanity.

Close your eyes and breathe the scent of your farm deeply.

—Beth

18. THE SUNSHINE HOUR

> Surely you have granted him unending blessings and made him glad with the joy of your presence.
>
> (Psalm 21:6)

Nearly one hundred years ago, a midwestern businessman, L. H. Turner, drove through a rural area near Terre Haute, Indiana. He saw a country church's windows and doors open and heard the strains of a harmonious quartet. He stopped to listen, and after hearing them perform, he asked them to participate in his local Sunday morning radio program for "the aged, blind, shut-ins, or incapacitated."

For fifty years, the quartet, along with various members of their families and others, carried the tradition of "The Sunshine Hour" weekly on secular radio station WBOW.

Launched on Easter morning in 1931 by Turner, the program was ultimately tagged the longest-running, live, non-denominational national radio program on Sunday mornings in the US.

The mission was to reach those who couldn't attend the church of their choosing and was foremost in the minds of Turner, the Gormong and Hayhurst farming families, and others who provided instrumental and vocal music, inspirational readings, and prayer. William W. Walford's memorable hymn, "Sweet Hour of Prayer," and Jeremiah E. Rankin's, "God Be with You," began and ended the program.

Turner focused on serving. The radio station furnished the hour for free but did not compensate him. Monetary donations were used to buy folding wheelchairs to loan to the needy.

The commitment to this weekly ministry was deeply entrenched in the Charles Gormong and Kendall Hayhurst's families—who were cousins. The families rose early to complete farm chores, head to WBOW for the program, and then attend their church in Prairie Creek.

Betty Jo Hayhurst, Kendall's daughter-in-law, remembers Saturday evenings were always uplifting and full of joy and laughter as they rehearsed the program at Kendall and his wife, Inez's, home. The families also involved their children, who played various instruments, sang, and served as program technicians.

Lord, "till we meet, till we meet, till we meet at Jesus's feet" are such precious words as we seek your face in person.

Sing your favorite hymn today and imagine sitting at Jesus's feet.

—Susan

19. FARM MEALS WITH RITA

> Every day they continued to meet together in the temple courts. They broke bread in their homes and ate together with glad and sincere hearts, praising God and enjoying the favor of all the people. And the Lord added to their number daily those who were being saved.
>
> (Acts 2:46–47)

My mother-in-law, Rita, was a fantastic cook. My favorite meal was her vegetable soup. Of course, like any good Midwesterner, vegetable soup started with ground beef. I was surprised the first time I took a bite to find meat among the veggies in my spoon. False advertising, if you ask me. Shouldn't the soup have been named Ground Beef and Vegetable Soup?

But I didn't name it, nor was I opposed to eating the savory creation. Potatoes, corn, green beans, onions, tomatoes, cabbage, and mushroom—plus the browned ground beef—were all simmered on low for a long time, flavors melding together into a mouthwatering creation.

Oh, the smell when entering Rita's house for lunch. Heavenly. We'd all squish around her tiny kitchen table, elbows hitting, knees bumping, spoons clinking off bowls. Laughter, stories of the morning's work, sometimes arguments about what to do in the afternoon, but always kisses for grandbabies and butter on crackers.

Eating together, while all knotted up around the table, are some of the best farm memories I have. When Rita died, her recipes died with her. They all came from a rote memory that years of experience provided—no cookbook or recipe card needed. But most importantly, she made her meals with love. The recipes started in her heart before traveling to her head and hands.

I'm thankful for those family meals, and I'm grateful for the ones we still have, even though one seat is empty. Rita taught us the value of family and taking time to sit down for a good meal and enjoy each other's company.

Lord, thank you for those who love and loved us well. Bring their faces to our minds today as we stop to feed our bodies.

Do you have a favorite family meal? What special memories surround that dish?

—Beth

20. DESIRE IS BY DESIGN

> 'For I know the plans I have for you,' declares the Lord, 'plans to prosper you and not to harm you, plans to give you hope and a future. Then you will call upon me and come and pray to me, and I will listen to you. You will seek me and find me when you seek me with all your heart.'
>
> (Jeremiah 29:11–13)

How do you know when your heart's vocational desire is valid?

Although I have been a writer for diverse audiences for many years, I questioned that desire. I wanted, even craved, the validity that the Lord wanted me to write and often prayed, "Please, Lord, show me your will. I love writing but is that what you want for me?"

Several years ago, while driving to an agriculture writing conference, I was listening to a call-in talk show on a Christian radio station. The show's guest was Christian writer and songwriter Michael Card. I decided to call in.

When the station answered and said I was in the queue to talk to Michael, I almost veered off the road. Suddenly I hear, "Susan, this is Michael Card. What's your question?"

"I love to write but don't know if that's what God wants me to do. How do I know God's desire?"

"Susan, I think it's intentional that you're writing. Your yearning is by God's design. Keep writing. It honors him."

I remember thanking him, hanging up, and crying. The brief conversation was such an incredible answer to prayer.

Our pastor recently said everything we do, including our vocations, is worship to the Lord.

God, our provider, help us to seek you with open hearts and wait expectantly for the answer. Amen.

Have you given your heart's desires to the Lord? If not, what are you waiting for?

—Susan

21. BAD BOY BUGGY

> Very early in the morning, while it was still dark, Jesus got up, left the house and went off to a solitary place, where he prayed.
>
> (Mark 1:35)

"Can I go for a ride with Nanny?" Four-year-old Jaena bounced with excitement in front of me. I had watched the golf cart coming up the road and was ready for the question.

"Put on your shoes first." My daughter could care less about her shoes but dutifully slipped them on and ran out the back door. I watched Jeana jump on the golf cart and snuggle up in her grandmother's big hug before they took off for the farm. Jaena was the first grandchild and a much-desired granddaughter after her grandmother had raised three sons.

Nanny, otherwise known as Rita, my mother-in-law, had recently bought a golf cart and christened her new ride the Bad Boy Buggy. She stenciled flowers on the sides and began giving Jaena rides. Nanny would drive back and forth between her house and mine, picking up Jaena and taking her home to play and share freezer pops.

Rides with Nanny were special occasions. They were slow rides down corn-lined roads ... a grandma with her first granddaughter ... moments my daughter treasured.

God also cherishes his time with us, which means we sometimes need to slow down. He wants nothing more than to be with us, his beloved children. Sometimes when I get into the car to come home after work, I purposely leave the radio off, roll the window down, and spend some time in prayer. What a precious time alone with God, my friend and creator.

Lord, you often went off to be alone with the Father. Remind us to do the same.

Find a few minutes today to slow down and spend time with God.

—Beth

22. GREEN ACRES, HOOSIER STYLE

> Rejoice in the Lord always. I will say it again: Rejoice!
> (Philippians 4:4)

My late godmother always promised me one day I would marry my "prince." Since I was a little girl, I envisioned having a fairy-tale wedding, marrying a tall, handsome man who worked a nine-to-five job, and living in a beautiful home in a big city.

God has a great sense of humor. I met my husband, Terry, through a blind date for my tenth high school reunion. My girlfriend, who knew me well, arranged the date. (Yes, we are still friends!) I was dismayed when I found out he was a farmer. I was allergic to everything he represented.

After a four-month courtship, tall and handsome Terry proposed, and blinded by love, I said, "Yes." Our fairy-tale wedding included a reception at our alma mater's Purdue Memorial Union. Our tongue-in-cheek wedding theme song was from the television show, "Green Acres."

Being a city girl, I liked to think I favored actress Ava Gabor (Lisa Douglas) with her fancy clothes and feathery slippers. Farmer Terry was a casual version of actor Eddie Albert (Oliver Douglas). "Farm living is the life for me" is

Terry's favorite part of the theme song.

Farm living, which has never been nine-to-five during our marriage, has been my husband's God-given passion since he was fourteen. I enjoy my occasional city girl "fix" but embrace my cozy slipper socks while sitting on the porch talking to our Hereford cows in the pasture.

Living in an old farmhouse does not rival a high rise in New York City. I have sat on electric fences and popped a wheelie driving a tractor. These experiences only bring laughter at the moment.

It took a long time to overcome culture shock, but the Lord led me to seek his joy in whatever I encountered while living the farm life.

Dear Lord, you knew before you created the world my mate would be a farmer. What joy that must have given you, as it now gives me. In your name, Amen.

Try to remember times when the Lord surprised you with joy. Create joy for someone else this week.

—Susan

PEACE

But the fruit of the Spirit is love, joy, peace, forbearance, kindness, goodness, faithfulness, gentleness and self-control. Against such things there is no law.

—Galatians 5:22–23

23. EARLY MORNING/LATE NIGHT

> Now may the Lord of peace himself give you peace at all times and in every way. The Lord be with all of you.
> (2 Thessalonians 3:16)

"I'm working late. Don't stay up." Another late night. *I wish he'd let me know earlier.* I huffed as I realized I'd stayed up way past bedtime, waiting on Jeff for no good reason. I turned off the television and headed for bed.

Hours later, I woke and rolled over to see the clock's red digital numbers light up the night. Three in the morning. No Jeff. Instant fear gripped my chest. *Where is he? Surely he's not still harvesting? Is he okay?*

I grabbed my phone to check the location app telling me where he—or at least his phone—was. GPS placed him in the farm office. I called his number while praying that he would answer.

"I'm okay."

"Are you okay?"

We both spoke at the same time.

"Just finishing up paperwork. I'll be home in a few."

I could hear the exhaustion in his voice, but I was relieved to know he'd safely finished another long day of harvesting. I wish this had been a one-time event, but, as any farm spouse knows, many long days and nights occur during planting and harvesting seasons. We all know those moments when our hearts drop into our chests, and our breathing becomes shallow as we realize something might possibly have gone wrong. Yet, in those moments, we are reminded of what and who is important. Minor irritations fade away. Disagreements resolve without words. And we are thankful for each other.

In the irritating moments of marriage, I wish I could remember the feeling of relief that comes after a big scare. And in the frightening moments, I'm thankful God is the Lord of peace, promising he is watching over us in every situation and moment.

Lord, you are the provider of peace, the guardian of our loved ones, and the omnipresent one in our lives. Help us remember what is truly important: our love for each other and your presence in all situations.

When you pray for safety on the farm, also pray for the Lord's peace in your heart and relationships.

—Beth

24. FERTILIZE YOUR MIND

Test me, O Lord, and try me, examine my heart and my mind; for I have always been mindful of your unfailing love and have lived in reliance on your faithfulness.

(Psalm 26:2–3)

I have always been a voracious reader. My parents and I religiously read the newspaper, including the funnies, every morning during breakfast. As a child, I could digest two Nancy Drew books daily.

When I was a teenager, I gravitated to *Seventeen* and *Glamour* magazines. As a young, single professional living in Indianapolis, my friends and I traded *Indianapolis Monthly* magazines. Little did I know how radically my reading materials would change.

When my husband, Terry, and I became engaged, my boss at the Purdue Alumni Association suggested I ask Terry for some of his farming publications so I could stay abreast of what he was talking about on our nightly phone calls. Stacks of magazines and newspapers came my way. I became familiar with *Indiana Prairie Farmer*, *Farmworld*, and *Successful Farming*.

Shortly after we married, the rental of a hog facility became available. Suddenly, our coffee table displayed not only *Midwest Living* and *Bon Appetit* but *National Hog*

Farmer and *Manure Manager*. I love my husband, but my magazine choices shocked my city-living girlfriends.

While my choice of reading materials was for entertainment or self-improvement, these informational periodicals were valuable to Terry for the growth and betterment of our farming operation.

Do I still read *Indianapolis Monthly*? Occasionally. Am I enthralled by *Manure Manager*? Definitely not! Now, together, Terry and I pore over *Hereford World* to learn how we can improve our cattle herd. We read the Bible together and discuss what we study. The Word fortifies our faith, stirs our spirits, and spurs us on to be the Lord's servants.

Just as Terry prioritizes using the proper implements for our operation and various forms of fertilizer on our fields to produce bountiful and healthy crops, so we enrich our lives daily with God's Word to grow the fruit of his Spirit.

What has the place of honor on your coffee table?

Heavenly Father, may Colossians 3:16, "Let the message of Christ dwell among you richly," be a life verse for us all.

Review your favorite books and magazines. Are they cultivating your spiritual life in the Lord?

—Susan

25. THERE'S A TICK ON MY BACK

> Do not be anxious about anything, but in every situation, by prayer and petition, with thanksgiving, present your requests to God. And the peace of God, which transcends all understanding, will guard your hearts and your minds in Christ Jesus.
>
> (Philippians 4:6-7)

We had gone to bed for the night. Jeff had just started snoring when I felt something crawl across my back. I let out a bloodcurdling scream.

"Something's on my back!"

Jeff bolted upright and flipped on the light, ready to kill any intruder threatening my life.

"What? What's wrong?" He rubbed his eyes in confusion.

How was I to know? I couldn't see what was on my back. That's why I was yelling for him.

"A bug, a spider. I don't know, but something's crawling up my back!" I had a full case of the heebie-jeebies going.

"Relax. It's just a tick." Jeff reached over and plucked the disgusting intruder off.

After much searching through sheets, covers, and pillows, I moved on to brushing my hair before determining the tick had no little friends hanging around. I relaxed enough to turn off the lights, but found sleep took quite a while longer to come.

It's incredible how such a small creature can shatter a peaceful night's sleep.

I'm thankful that when I have little ticks of worry keeping me up at night, God can pick them off and throw them away. I just need to ask him and trust that he will provide the required peace.

Lord, thank you for your peace that passes all understanding amid our anxious moments.

Are anxious thoughts causing you restlessness? Ask God for his peace today.

—Beth

26. BLOOM WHERE YOU ARE PLANTED

I can do all this through him who gives me strength.

(Philippians 4:13)

I first read the phrase, "bloom where you are planted," in my junior high art classroom. I didn't really understand the saying until my way of life changed when I married my farmer, Terry, and experienced a major culture shock in every possible way.

Marrying Terry was not the issue—he was a saint to put up with my tears, frustrations, loneliness, and depression for many years. While one of our wedding scriptures was Ruth 1:16, "Where you go, I will go, and where you stay, I will stay. Your people will be my people and your God my God," I had a hard time accepting the alterations.

Terry grew up Pilgrim Holiness/Wesleyan. I grew up Presbyterian. He lived with his parents on a farm eight miles from town. I lived in an apartment in a historic mansion. Terry was outside all day getting dirty, and I worked at my inside dream job. While he was content to stay at home for weeks at a time, I thrived on activity.

Thank goodness our faith in the Lord knitted us together from the beginning. People who knew me well provided good advice: "Get active in the community." "Find a woman's Bible study." "Make friends through work." "Pray for another farm wife to give you pointers on your new life."

Their suggestions helped, but I'm still a work in progress over the culture shock. The best lessons were advocating and writing for agriculture, teaching our daughters to be proud of their heritage, and trusting in the Lord daily to show me how to adapt.

Am I blooming where I've been planted? During our nearly thirty-five years of marriage, I have embraced being an enthusiastic spokesperson for the agricultural industry. I know how to plug into my environment. Some days as I wash manure-covered laundry, I wish I still lived in the city where streets are paved and activity reigns. Then, as I gaze at another sunset painted by the Lord himself, I try to plant myself deeper right where I am.

Thank goodness, Lord, for your unlimited strength that gives us victory.

The Word calls us to be content and grateful. Where do you need to better bloom where God plants you?

—Susan

27. THE CASE OF THE MISSING DOORKNOB

In the same way, the Spirit helps us in our weakness. We do not know what we ought to pray for, but the Spirit himself intercedes for us through wordless groans.

(Romans 8:26)

Trips to Grandma and Grandpa Johnson's farm in eastern Indiana filled my childhood. Their old white farmhouse stood at the top of a long gravel drive. They had stacked toys and jigsaw puzzles in one of the upstairs closets, awaiting grandchildren to play with them.

One day, I made a startling discovery after playing with my favorite puzzle. The doorknob was missing, and I was locked inside.

I saw my mom's high school photo atop a dresser. "Mom, help," I sobbed, panicking. *I'll be here forever. I'm stuck in here until I die.* I pulled her photo to my chest and curled into a ball on the floor.

After what felt like an eternity, I heard a door slam and the rush of water from the kitchen sink. I realized I was lying next to a metal grate. Cool air from the room below hit my face when I leaned over its open slats. I could hear Grandma humming in the kitchen.

"Help," I whispered. "Help," I got a little louder. "Help, I'm stuck," I roared into the grate. A moment later, Grandma was looking up at me.

"You're stuck, how?"

"The doorknob. It's gone."

Grandma rushed up the stairs. Soon the bedroom door swung open, and she wrapped me in her safe, strong arms.

Panic threatens us sometimes. And while we can see no solution, God has one. He isn't standing in the kitchen under the grate. He is even closer. And we don't have to yell to get his attention. All we need to do is cry out to him, even if it's only a whispered "help." Even if we utter a silent prayer, he hears.

Lord, thank you for hearing our prayers, even when we can't form the words. Amen.

When you find you're in need today, call out to God.

—Beth

28. ACT OF OBEDIENCE

> A wife of noble character who can be found? She is worth far more than rubies.
>
> (Proverbs 31:10)

The Proverbs 31 woman has always daunted, even intimidated, me. Verses 10–31 depict an ideal wife and mother whose traits make me feel overwhelmed and exhausted just by reading about them. Who in the world can live up to those expectations? What if the Lord, through Solomon, encourages us to consider the gifts and talents he's given us and how to use them as farmers and farmwives?

I remember listening to my pastor read Proverbs 3. Verses that remind me of farm life struck me. Verse eleven sets the woman's course: "Her husband has full confidence in her and lacks nothing of value." My husband, Terry, assures me he has trust in me even when I back the livestock trailer into a fence. Verse fourteen says, "She is like the merchant ships, bringing her food from afar." I don't like being compared to a ship, but I know my family appreciates bagged lunches and hot sandwiches in the evenings when they work late in the fields.

I growl when reading part of verse fifteen: "She gets up while it is still night." While Terry wakes up at five, I am not a morning person. However, I know a hearty breakfast helps him start vigorously.

Terry's favorite verse is sixteen: "She considers a field and buys it." He's still waiting for me to buy him a field, but I occasionally advocate for buying a new combine.

I cherish verse twenty-three: "Her husband is respected at the city gate, where he takes his seat among the elders of the land." God wants me to be grateful for Terry's leadership position as the head of our farm. But, most importantly, I'm challenged to pray for him daily for strength, endurance, and humility.

Are we conscientious and faithful? Do we fear and worship the Lord? These are acts of obedience to the Lord characterized in Proverbs 31.

Lord, as women, we often feel overwhelmed and underappreciated. Help us to better understand our worth and see our value through your eyes.

Read Psalm 31:10–31 slowly and pray over how you can better accomplish the path before you.

—Susan

29. RESTING BY THE ROAD

> Come to me, all you who are weary and burdened, and I will give you rest.
>
> (Matthew 11:28)

I drove slowly down the dirt road, attempting to keep the toddlers behind me asleep in their car seats. I parked at the edge of the road and watched Jeff's combine head away from me. His lunch box sat on the seat next to me.

"Thank you, Jesus." I reclined my seat into the resting position, closed my eyes, and took a deep, relaxing breath. I knew my husband wouldn't see me until he reached the end and turned the combine around to head back. *Maybe I'd even get a five-minute nap.*

As the mother of three girls under five, the only peaceful time of the day happened when I delivered meals to Jeff. The girls were trapped in seat belts. Working on my to-do list was impossible. All I could do was sit and wait. That day, I had sent up a prayerful plea that Jeff would take a long time to get his lunch.

During harvest season, Jeff spent most of the daytime hours in the combine, and I became a single mom. I needed that noon nap to help me survive the rest of the day. I would be in charge of changing diapers, feeding meals, bathing, and bedtime routine. Survival meant grabbing peaceful moments wherever I could find them.

Are you weary? Do you need rest? Do you feel as if you work from sunup to sundown? Ask God to show you quiet times hidden in the middle of the day's busyness, even if it's only a couple of minutes while the kids are buckled securely in their car seats.

Lord, give us your strength in busy times, but also help us see the hidden opportunities to rest today.

Where and when can you carve out time to rest today?

—Beth

30. THE CROSS TERRY BUILT

> You will keep in perfect peace those whose minds are steadfast, because they trust in you.
>
> (Isaiah 26:3)

Everyone knows weddings can be stressful and chaotic. Throw in having one at your home or farm, and the anxiety levels skyrocket. Honey-do lists are the length of a college term paper, the house and the machinery shed must be power-washed, and you accept the neighbor's offer to put in new landscaping in exchange for freezer pork. Prayer became my mainstay.

While COVID-19 derailed our daughter Lillian's plans for a big church wedding, the pandemic also brought unexpected blessings. My husband, Terry, and I encouraged Lillian and her husband Kegan to cancel the church and drop from three hundred to one hundred guests.

Our daughter's next request was if they could have the wedding and reception at the farm. Terry said "yes"—if he could make them a cross for the ceremony in our yard. The kids loved the idea.

One morning, I heard the noise of the skid steer and voices outside my bedroom window. Terry and Kegan were knocking down two old canning sheds and cleaning off the site. I heard Terry pounding and hammering near the same window the following morning. He came in a few hours later and said, "Honey, it's done. Go look at it."

Terry had fashioned some of the shed's wooden beams into a beautiful twelve-by-eight-foot-wide cross. As I walked up to it, I broke into tears. The Lord spoke to my heart, saying, "This is what it's all about. I am the center of the marriage and the wedding. It's all about me."

Truer words were never spoken. The wedding, reception, and Sunday brunch went off without a hitch. The couple is happily married. The cross stands permanently in the center of our yard, reminding our family that the Lord and Savior Jesus Christ controls everything.

Immanuel, why do I ever doubt you? Your ways are excellent and masterful. Your peace flows like a river. Thank you.

What concerns do you need to release to the Lord, the provider of all things? Seek him and be awed by his answers.

—Susan

31. EAGLES OVERHEAD

But those who hope in the Lord will renew their strength. They will soar on wings like eagles; they will run and not grow weary, they will walk and not be faint.

(Isaiah 40:31)

One of my favorite parts of country life is seeing the wildlife make their home in the nearby woods. I recognize the destructive power of deer when they make a cornfield their home, and the howling coyotes make an eerie sound.

But I enjoy the sight of a fox, rabbit, or wild turkey as I drive toward home. My favorite part of nature is the bird sounds in the early morning when they wake the world with their comforting songs. I placed a bird feeder right outside my kitchen window so I could join them for breakfast. Finches, robins, cardinals, blue jays, and woodpeckers share their morning routine with me. A pair of doves makes a nest in the roofline every spring.

A couple of years ago, an eagle, the most magnificent of birds, decided to nest just across the road. Watching the power course through the bird of prey's expansive wings as he soared effortlessly above our home awed me.

Isaiah's words bring comfort when he tells us if we place our hope in God, he will renew our strength to do the difficult work before us. We won't literally fly through the sky like the eagles, although I wish I could, but God will give us the strength for each task. We can move through our days peacefully, knowing God renews our strength daily.

Lord, renew my strength as I work to accomplish all that needs doing today.

Name a time when God gave you renewed strength to finish a difficult task.

—Beth

32. MINISTRY TO FARM

> Therefore, as we have opportunity, let us do good to all people.
>
> (Galatians 6:10)

Moving to the farm was supposed to be temporary—at least that's what we thought. Jeff had a degree in Christian Ministries and was an ordained pastor. The plan was to help his dad for a little while, and then we would be back in ministry. But soon, the months turned to a year, and a year turned to two.

"Are you going to start looking for a church position?" I eased the question into conversation one day.

"I enjoy working at the farm and volunteering at church. I think I'm where I'm supposed to be right now."

Jeff's answer didn't surprise me. I could tell he was happy, but I realized I needed to spend time in prayer regarding my call to ministry. I assumed that marrying a preacher was how I would fulfill the desire for ministry I had felt as a teenager.

God and I had some talking to do. At first, I questioned God. *How could this be your will for my life?* I wish the questioning had taken weeks or months, but I was hardheaded. But, over many years, I have understood that ministry is a lifestyle, not only an occupation.

During our twenty-six years on the farm, God has used us as volunteer ministers—ways he could never have used us if we weren't living on a farm. We provided backhoes, tractors, and combines to other farmers in need, watched neighbor's children during moments of crisis, and prayed with hurting farm friends.

I learned ministry doesn't exist only inside church walls or on a mission field in a distant county. Charity can happen in the middle of a soybean field. Ministry is as close as my back door.

Lord, open our eyes to opportunities to show your love to all we encounter.

Write down the name of someone you feel God is asking you to help.

—Beth

PATIENCE

But the fruit of the Spirit is love, joy, peace, forbearance, kindness, goodness, faithfulness, gentleness and self-control. Against such things there is no law.

—Galatians 5:22–23

33. RAIN, GO AWAY; RAIN, COME BACK

> You care for the land and water it; you enrich it abundantly. The streams of God are filled with water to provide the people with grain, for so you have ordained it. You drench its furrows and level its ridges; you soften it with showers and bless its crops. You crown the year with your bounty, and your carts overflow with abundance.
>
> (Psalm 65:9–11)

During the month of May, rain fell day after day. As soon as the ground dried enough to plant, a new storm popped up again. Farmers all over the area worried and gathered to commiserate during the planting season. Eventually, all the seeds found their way into the soil.

Then the rain stopped. Once again, the local farmers fretted and complained. After hearing so much gloomy talk, I began my campaign of anxiety.

"Jeff, what'll we do? The forecast looks horrible this year." I flopped down on the couch at the end of another hot, dry day.

"Dad always says, 'We've never not had a crop. Some years are better than others. But there's always crops to pick.'"

I slept a little better that night and tried to worry less. Sure enough, the bins were full at the end of the harvest season, perhaps not overflowing, but we received fruit from our labor—or should I say corn and soybeans.

I learned that year to trust God even when the weather doesn't cooperate with our plans. Throughout the years of farming, we've never had a perfect year. But God has always provided when we've done our work—planting and harvesting through the less-than-ideal days and leaning on him to calm our anxious minds.

Lord, teach us to trust in you and be patient in life's imperfections.

Next time you find yourself complaining or worrying, ask God for patience to trust he will provide.

—Beth

34. THE DADDY MONTHS

> Love the Lord your God with all your heart and with all your soul and with all your strength. These commandments that I give you today are to be on your hearts. Impress them on your children. Talk about them when you sit at home and when you walk along the road, when you lie down and when you get up.
>
> (Deuteronomy 6:5–7)

Family time on the farm sometimes comes at a premium because of planting and harvesting schedules, livestock work, or running side businesses. How did we find that coveted and cherished family time? Enter the Daddy months.

When our daughters, Lillian and Hayley, were young, we had a weaner-to-finish hog operation, along with our row crops and Herefords. My husband's time involved long and late hours. Upon reviewing our annual calendars and farm rhythms, I coined the phrase "the Daddy months"—a reference to December to February, when his schedule was lighter.

Those special months began the day after harvest. Lillian vividly remembers when our pace slowed down. "Daddy was able to be in for dinner and be with us girls and the cattle more. Mom was less stressed. Daddy was more relaxed, enjoyed the fireplace, and took daytime naps. I loved watching him and Bop (Terry's dad) work on old tractors. We loved riding with him in the tractors in the winter and listening to *Adventures in Odyssey* and *The Sunshine Hour*."

Hayley waited expectantly for board games, eating together at the dining table, decorating Christmas sugar cookies with lots of frosting, and trips to Rural King for farm supplies and free popcorn.

Terry also prioritized dates with the girls, individually and together. He took them out to lunch, for ride-alongs in the semi while hauling grain, and on trips to deliver cattle to the processor.

Terry's most treasured time throughout the years was teaching the girls' Sunday school class. He poured the Word into them and encouraged them to ask probing questions and think reflectively on Scripture.

The Daddy months impressed upon the girls their father's love and dedication for them.

Abba, Father, you are our daddy, always available, always with us. I praise you for being one of your cherished children.

Can you carve out a dedicated time of year for your loved ones? What would that look like?

—Susan

35. TRACTOR NAPPING

Be joyful in hope, patient in affliction, faithful in prayer.
(Romans 12:12)

One day Jeff took our two younger girls with him in the tractor to give me a much-needed break.

"Jess is too close, Dad." The two young girls wiggled in the cramped buddy seat, trying to get comfortable.

"You'll be all right. She'll be asleep in a few minutes."

"That's what I'm afraid of," Jo mumbled, irritated at having to share the seat and her dad with her "baby" sister.

Soon the toddler had drifted off, and Jo and Jeff rode in peaceful silence ... for a few minutes.

"Dad! She peed on me!" Jo was livid. "I knew she would!"

Jeff made a quick phone call, ending my precious alone time. I closed the book I was reading, grabbed some towels, and headed to the tractor. Once home, both girls went straight into the bathtub—the day heading in a different direction than any of us wanted.

How does our modern version of the line from Robert Burn's poem "To a Mouse" go? "The best-laid plans of mice and men often go awry."

Sometimes, our idea of how our days will go doesn't work out as desired. Jeff tells me, "Don't ask me where I will be. Call when you're ready to come, and I'll tell you where I am. The plan could change at any moment."

We need the skill to pivot and improvise when a crisis happens or a project bumps its way up to the highest priority. Attaining this skill is easier said than done, but with prayer and God's help, we can face the day with patience and grace.

Lord, help me meet today with an adaptable mind, a patient demeanor, and a good sense of humor.

How have you seen God help you in irritating or unexpected situations?

—Beth

36. YOUR PRAYER CLOSET

> But when you pray, go into your room, close the door and pray to your Father, who is unseen. Then your Father, who sees what is done in secret, will reward you.
>
> (Matthew 6:6)

Do you remember your mom or grandmother wearing an apron while they cooked or cleaned? Do you know why aprons were worn?

Aprons were a practical necessity in the early 1800s. Women didn't own many dresses. They washed clothes minimally, so aprons protected women's dresses.

The 1920s and '30s brought handmade aprons made from sacks containing seed or flour. By the 1940s and '50s, the half apron became popular—many made from feminine prints and adorned with pockets and frilly trims.

According to www.sharonglasgow.com, women used aprons for countless reasons: as a potholder to remove hot pans from ovens, to carry eggs and chicks from the chicken coop, to transport fallen apples from the trees, and to wave so the men would know it was time to come in from the fields for dinner.

I have fond memories of my mom and paternal grandma wearing aprons as they cooked together in the kitchen and prepared sumptuous holiday meals.

Perhaps the most meaningful apron story I've read is that of Susanna Wesley, mother of noted sons John and Charles Wesley. She had nineteen children, with ten surviving. Susanna had her hands full, raising the family primarily by herself, as her husband, a pastor, traveled frequently.

She promised the Lord she would pray two hours a day, but like any mom, she struggled to find a quiet place to retreat. Susanna creatively made do and advised her children that when they saw her with her apron over her head, she was praying and should not be disturbed.

Her apron was her prayer closet. No matter her daily schedule of homeschooling her children, administering discipline, and teaching them manners, Susanna devoted herself to Christ, prayed for her children, absorbed the Word, and honored her Lord.

Father, help me faithfully dedicate quiet time with you daily. Lead me to the prayer closet you have for me.

How and when do you seek the Lord daily? Pray that he reveals himself to you.

—Susan

37. WATCH THE ROAD

> And over all these virtues put on love, which binds them all together in perfect unity. Let the peace of Christ rule in your hearts, since as members of one body you were called to peace. And be thankful.
>
> (Colossians 3:14–15)

"Watch the road!" I pushed down on my passenger-side imaginary brake and death-gripped the hand rest.

"Sorry."

Jeff swerved back between the white lines. But soon, his eyes roamed the passing fields again, and I gritted my teeth as tires hit the rumble strip, alerting us to the edge of the road.

I dreaded those afternoon drives. If the car wasn't swerving down the road, it was slowly weaving in and out of dealer parking lots while Jeff talked on the phone to his father about possible purchases. The definition of a drive with Jeff meant boredom interlaced with moments of fearing for my life.

My favorite pastime, reading, made me nauseous. Eventually, I found a hobby that took my mind off the distracted driving and gave me something fun to do while my farmer checked out the newest equipment available. I learned to knit.

On the way home from church one week, I noticed Jeff taking an unusual route.

"Mind if I check out the crops on the way home?" he asked after turning in the opposite direction from home.

"Go ahead. I can knit here just as well as I knit at home." I pulled out my needles and settled back in for a long drive home. We've come to a comfortable agreement on how to spend our afternoons.

Lord, help us find unity and joy in being together, despite our differences.

How do you carve out time together with those you love? In what ways do you bridge conflicting goals to create unity?

—Beth

38. KEEPING A SENSE OF HUMOR

> For the joy of the Lord is your strength.
>
> (Nehemiah 8:10)

On many days, my kitchen-window view provides surprises, one of which was attention-deficit cattle breaking through electric fences and galloping down the road. I lifted an urgent prayer for the Lord's strength. Then, I threw on a coat and grabbed my farm shoes, phone, and car keys. By then, those large, ornery bovines had sauntered through one neighbor's yard and crossed another road. Traversing a landlord's field and hightailing it over a third road brought the escaped cattle to a long open stretch of land with a tree line in the distance. Have I mentioned the temperature was frigid?

Lugging a bucket of grain to tempt them was a moot point in this journey. I called my husband Terry, who was seven miles away picking corn. He had to finish loading and hauling grain to the elevator before returning home. Grrrr.

Our New Holland Rustler was pinned in the machinery shed. Grrrr.

While I wanted to use our New Holland Rustler, I couldn't get to it in the machinery shed. More growling noises emerged from my mouth. I jumped in our van and called on nearby recruits. Helpers with feed buckets and farm vehicles followed the cows' trail and warded them off at various passes.

Every time Terry's cousin Larry and I drove alongside each other to check in, his nine-year-old exuberant granddaughter, Jena, would put her window down and say, "Isn't this fun?"

Larry's curt reply was always, "Put that window up!"

Terry showed up later, unearthed the Rustler, and prodded the cattle back to the home farm and into a pasture. The runaway cattle's total trip: two and one-half miles over rough Indiana farmland.

While I dream of escape-proof new fencing for our errant cattle, I'm reminded the Lord brings humor in our most trying situations. Sometimes, those circumstances comes with much-needed exercise. But, often, he brings comic relief through young children who experience sheer joy in a challenging situation.

Dear Jesus, I'm so glad you showed us laughter by bringing children along to see the joy in difficult circumstances.

Recount frustrating situations and dig in to discover joy-filled moments.

—Susan

39. THE CASE OF THE MOUSE IN THE OIL BOTTLE

> A cheerful heart is good medicine, but a crushed spirit dries up the bones.
>
> (Proverbs 17:22)

When we first moved to the farm, my family all made trips to visit us. I was excited to show off my little farmhouse and was thrilled to host them.

"Watch out for bugs, mice, and snakes," my dad and brother gently razzed me.

I shook off their warnings as fun teasing. But the day after they left, I opened the kitchen cabinet and found a mouse "swimming" in the vegetable-oil bottle. I grabbed my phone.

"Dad, did you put a mouse in my oil?"

"It wasn't me. Ask your brother."

"No, I didn't do it. Could the mouse have climbed in there?" I heard laughter in his voice.

"What? Like it climbed in and screwed the lid back on from the inside?"

I smiled, voicing my sarcasm at the incredulity of the statement, while still feeling slightly sick to my stomach whenever I looked at the bottle. I knew the two pranksters in the family had pranked me, but to this day, no one has taken credit for the deed.

Is your family like mine? Are there jokes and stories that bring laughter when retold? Are there pranks that leave you shaking your head?

Sometimes, we just have to shake our heads at the silly stunts our families pull for a good joke. Once we get over the shock of the prank, we have a story to tell for years to come. Laughter is good for the soul.

Lord, thank you for the times of laughter and good-natured fun we have with family.

Share a funny family memory today.

—Beth

40. MOVING ANTIQUES IN A LIVESTOCK TRAILER

> Watch out! Be on your guard against all kinds of greed; life does not consist in an abundance of possessions.
>
> (Luke 12:15)

Most people use a moving truck or a U-Haul trailer to move their precious belongings. However, my farmer offered his livestock trailer to move my family heirlooms.

I was stunned, appalled, and terrified—in that order. Stunned, because I'd never heard of such a thing. Appalled, because I knew that cattle manure was often found in every nook and cranny in the metal box. And terrified, because several of my grandma and mom's antiques would be traveling, hopefully secured, in that portable mode of transportation.

Terry and his best friend, Carl, scheduled my possessions' move from my apartment to our first home as newlyweds. I carefully wrapped every precious antique in blankets, sheets, and towels for protection. The guys used several ratchet straps to secure heavy pieces—a hide-a-bed, glass-topped dining room table, antique chairs, and bookshelves—to the inside of the trailer.

I pleaded for slow-driving speeds and no unnecessary rough roads or shortcuts. I am sure I held my breath for the two-hour drive.

Everything, except my nerves, safely arrived. The only piece of furniture that showed any damage was an antique chair my mom had reupholstered by hand. A grease streak marked the upper side of the chair's back. Spot cleaning didn't erase the stain. No matter where I have put the chair since then, I've made sure the stained side hugged a wall. Mom never knew about it.

Luke's parable of the rich fool in verses 13–21 recounts the man deciding he needed to build bigger barns to store his good crop. Then he rested on his laurels and celebrated. God admonished him, "You fool ... this is how it will be with anyone who stores up things for himself but is not rich toward God."

Do you spend more time garnering belongings than seeking the Lord daily?

Forgive me, Jesus, for placing things above you. Hold me accountable when pride infiltrates my soul. Amen.

Is pride an issue for you? Pray for a humble heart and a fresh connection with the Lord.

—Susan

41. YOU'RE DUE IN MAY?

> I remain confident of this: I will see the goodness of the Lord in the land of the living. Wait for the Lord; be strong and take heart and wait for the Lord.
>
> (Psalms 27:13–14)

"You're due in May?"

My father-in-law shook his head at the news—right in the middle of planting season. And sure enough, nine months later, on May 27, we gave them the news.

"It's a girl!" Rita, my mother-in-law, yelled out the van's window to my father-in-law, who was planting corn. The first grandchild made her appearance around noon on a sunny Monday.

Three weeks passed before they could drive to Michigan to hold baby Jaena. But Nanny and Pappy helped us move back to the farm a few days later, and Jaena was a quarter of a mile from their house for the rest of her childhood.

"Couldn't you plan any better?" I heard that question a few times, but evidently not. Our next two daughters came at busy farming times too. Daughter number two came in late March while we prepared for planting, and our youngest came in June, right at the end of the season.

With each delivery, I worried Jeff wouldn't be able to be there. But when each girl arrived, he was in the delivery room, and the planting happened, even if the schedule wasn't perfect.

Having babies is a beautiful, monumental moment in a couple's life. But their arrivals rarely follow our plans.

Like babies, I've learned God shows up at the perfect time, not always on my timetable. I must trust he knows best and will provide what I need when I need it, not when I want it.

Lord, your timetable is better than ours. Help us trust that you will provide at just the right moment in your goodness.

Where have you seen God's goodness delivered at an unexpected or unplanned time?

—Beth

42. WHAT'S A PLANNED VACATION?

> In their hearts humans plan their course, but the Lord determines their steps.
>
> (Proverbs 16:9)

My parents and grandparents frequently planned vacations. Since my farmer husband and I married, I, too, have aspired to organize planned getaways, although they are infused with unexpected, halted arrangements.

Terry's favorite travel anecdote (much to my dismay) is the two of us cruising implement dealerships on our drive from Sanibel Island, Florida, to Orlando while on our honeymoon.

When our daughters were young, I meticulously planned a weeklong vacation to Gatlinburg, Tennessee. The day before we were to leave, Terry announced we had weaner (high maintenance) pigs being delivered. Said trip was canceled. Later, trips to visit my parents in Florida were often nixed because of national cattle shows. I became frustrated and resentful.

Our girls were thrilled to join 4-H. My immediate response was, "Great, another thing to take away vacations."

My wise and dear friend, DeeDee, gently chastened me.

"Susan, those trips can come later. Embrace the wonderful experiences your family will have preparing your animals for the fair, completing projects, learning about 4-H, and participating in lots of fun and silliness. You will make unforgettable memories."

Her comments brought me up short but crystallized my new mission. Our getaways can occur in our community and at the state fair with friends and neighbors. While they still involved stocking up and eating out of coolers or at the 4-H Junior Leader stand, we spent time together as a family. We made heartfelt and innumerable memories.

Without my meticulous planning, the Lord blessed our girls with the opportunities to see other parts of the country. Lillian attended the National 4-H Congress in Atlanta, Georgia. Hayley spent her junior year away from Purdue University, studying at the Fashion Institute of Technology in New York City.

Trying to control can render us unable to reach for the Spirit's guidance. Proverbs 3:5–6 is my trusted reminder to get out of the way and listen to the Lord.

Heavenly Father, help us to trust you with all our hearts and lean not on our own understanding. Let us acknowledge you in all our ways so that you can make our paths straight.

In what ways do you need to release control today? The Lord has the answer.

—Susan

43. EXPERIENCED DRIVER

Therefore encourage one another and build each other up, just as in fact you are doing.

(1 Thessalonians 5:11)

When Jaena turned fifteen, we signed her up for Driver's Education. While she had been driving farm vehicles for a while, she needed the classroom instructions on road regulations for "normal" vehicles.

After the classroom portion, she needed driving time with an instructor to pass the class. On the beginning day, the teacher picked Jaena to drive first. She hopped in the car, fastened her seatbelt, checked her mirrors, and took off. She sped up gradually to the designated speed, turned correctly, and braked smoothly. No big deal.

When Jaena's turn was over, she traded spots with the next girl, who fumbled with the key and needed instructions on how to start the car. The untrained girl looked at the instructor with fear in her eyes.

"Don't worry. She's experienced," the instructor said, pointing at Jaena as he reassured the rest of the kids in the car.

One of the good things about farm life is the practical knowledge our children inherently learn. Farm life gives much knowledge and wisdom—whether it's the early experience with mechanics, the knowledge of the "birds and bees" from raising cows, understanding "life and death" through watching the life cycle of a sweet little piglet grow into a huge sow, or the seasonal cycles and its related weather.

With knowledge and wisdom comes the need for patience with others, like Jaena's driving instructor had with the other students in his car. While Jaena came home with a funny story, her instructor modeled Christ's patience with us when we needed instruction and guidance.

Lord, help me patiently and unconditionally accept those who are less knowledgeable or experienced.

Is God asking you to mentor someone? How can you show patience as you teach them?

—Beth

KINDNESS

But the fruit of the Spirit is love, joy, peace, forbearance, kindness, goodness, faithfulness, gentleness and self-control. Against such things there is no law.

—Galatians 5:22–23

44. CORNERED BY A BULL

The LORD is gracious and righteous; our God is full of compassion. The LORD protects the unwary; when I was brought low, he saved me.

(Psalm 116:5-6)

One of the highlights of my childhood was visiting my grandparents' farm. I was the youngest of their grandchildren, and they were retired by the time I came along.

We grandkids were given free run of the farm. There wasn't much danger we could get into with only a small pen of hogs and a couple of cows. But somehow, we managed to find where danger lurked. My older brother and cousin led the way, of course. (At least, that's my memory. Don't ask my brother. He may have a very different story to tell. Perhaps one about trying to get away from an annoying little sister.)

One day, we ran off to explore the pasture. The farther we got from Grandma's house, the farther behind I trailed. My little-girl legs couldn't keep up with their long, preteen ones. They reached the middle of the pasture just as I climbed up the fence to enter.

"Run!" they yelled.

I looked up to see the biggest bull I'd ever seen chasing them. I swung back over the fence to safety and was quickly followed by those, who moments before, I had envied for their speed. My slowness saved me, just as their quickness saved them. I've never forgotten that day, the first day I saw fear in my big brother's eyes.

Throughout life, we will face fear-producing situations and run up against enemies stronger than us. But we have a God who is bigger than our fears, whose power is made perfect in our weaknesses, and who gives us what we need in each situation.

Lord, thank you for your strength when I am weak, your power when I feel powerless, and your grace displayed in my life.

Where have you seen God's power displayed in fearful moments?

—Beth

45. PRODIGAL ANNIE

> But the father said to his servants, 'Quick ... Bring the fattened calf and kill it. Let's have a feast and celebrate. For this son of mine was dead and is alive again; he was lost and is found.' So, they began to celebrate.
>
> (Luke 15:22, 23–24)

Even cattle can be wayward. Our family has had our share of feisty Hereford cattle. One endearing calf was Annie Oakley. Since her birth in 2008, she has ingratiated herself to our family and friends. Each time I finished bottle feeding her supplement, she chased and nudged me for more. Annie followed us around the pasture, endlessly craving head and brisket scratches.

Her cuteness factor ended the day she walked through the electric fence, not once, but twelve times. One of those times, in the dark of the evening, I found Annie in our neighbor's yard. While I jumped into the van, my husband and daughters, fresh out of their evening showers, climbed into the Gator and headed down the road.

When they pulled up alongside Annie, she walked up to them and let them load her in the back. With Lillian holding Annie's back end, Terry put Annie's head in a headlock, and Hayley drove the Gator. Suddenly, I heard Lillian scream, "Mom, she just peed on us!" Two full-size cattle gates barricaded her in the barn until the following day.

Luke's account of the prodigal son details how the son had squandered his father's resources, ignored his father's love, groveled for food, and ate pig slop.

How often have I sidestepped fences put up for my good, spent money when I shouldn't, or put my desire for things first when my parents and the Lord set appropriate and wise boundaries? Have my parents always welcomed me back home? Yes, with hugs and encouragement. Has the Lord always gathered me into his arms? Yes, with wisdom from his Word and a reminder to repent and be forgiven.

Lord, how amazing to be celebrated as your child. Thank you.

Do you have wayward habits? Take them to your Father in prayer.

—Susan

46. LOCKED IN THE CAGE

> You hem me in behind and before, and you lay your hand upon me. Such knowledge is too wonderful for me, too lofty for me to attain.
>
> (Psalm 139:5–6)

"Mom locks us in the cage," my five-year-old daughter told the store clerk.

"Jaena, it's not a cage. It's the gate to our yard where your playhouse is. I lock the gate because we live next to the highway." I spoke the words more for the woman's sake than to inform Jaena.

The clerk smiled. I hoped she believed me and didn't call the police as soon as I walked away. I loved the fenced-in yard we'd created for our girls. There was an old chicken coop "playhouse." In the corner, a dogwood tree grew, providing hours of climbing fun and good shade for picnics. What a wonderful cage … I mean play yard.

The play yard got me thinking of times when I've felt caged in by God. I didn't plan to spend my life on a farm. I loved the idea of being a missionary, traveling to distant locations, and seeing the world. But God had other plans. He rooted me to this place, this farm. He caged me like my girls in their yard and the chickens before them in the old chicken coop.

I had to learn to see the blessing of being inside that cage: the nearness of family, the beautiful stars at night, the smell of freshly dug fields, and a husband working nearby.

Lord, I'm grateful for your hemming in. Help me see the blessings coming from the boundary lines you've placed in my life.

Next time you want to complain about feeling caged in, look around for the blessings instead.

—Beth

47. HELP! MY CHILD IS JOINING 4-H

Command them to do good, to be rich in good deeds, and to be generous and willing to share.

(1 Timothy 6:18)

Ribbons, projects, and deadlines, oh my.

My nine-year-old daughter, Lillian, had joined 4-H, the century-old youth organization where children forge friendships, learn about leadership and perseverance, and develop community service and organizational skills.

While Terry had been a local, state, and national 4-H award winner, I was not a hallowed 4-H alumnus and had no idea how to shepherd our daughters through the proposed ten-year maze.

What's a mom to do? Call in her personal calvary—4-H mom extraordinaire and friend, Karen, to break me in gently and set the stage. Karen was a veteran 4-H leader. With notebook and pen in hand, I took copious notes throughout our two-hour conversation, preparing myself to help Lillian and Hayley with their myriad tasks.

During my education process, Karen inspired me to have my girls create individual categorized totes for their projects and me to have my 4-H-will-travel toolbox. My storage container sported must-haves, including wire cutters, duct tape, various sized plastic bags, project hanging and poster tags, and black sharpies.

Did I mention my learning curve was bathed in prayer? Our family's Scripture life verse, Philippians 4:13, "I can do all this though him who gives me strength," bolstered all of us.

What started as an anxiety-filled, tearful dialogue with Karen concluded thirteen years later with two confident young adults, prepped with life skills learned in 4-H. More importantly, their thriving years in the organization enhanced their God-given passions. Lillian's commitment to agriculture brought her and her husband, Kegan, into our farming operation. Hayley started sewing during her first year in 4-H and now works in the fashion industry in England.

Ribbons are thrilling, projects are demanding, and deadlines are nerve-racking. But the Lord knew what he was doing when 4-H became a part of the Hayhurst family. We made lifelong memories, sharpened our skills, and substantiated passions. And God reminded this mom that she could do all things through Jesus.

Dear Lord, thank you for dear friends who rescue us and for precious times with my daughters.

If you're a seasoned volunteer, pray how you might mentor others who need your expertise.

—Susan

48. SAVING STRAY CATS

> But when the kindness and love of God our Savior appeared, he saved us, not because of righteous things we had done, but because of his mercy.
>
> (Titus 3:4–5)

Jeff came home on a frigid winter night with the news that a mama cat had abandoned her three kittens.

"I found three kittens down at the farm. The momma cat must have abandoned them. With the freezing weather tonight, they may not survive. Do you want them?"

What a silly question. I had lost my two cats to old age a few years earlier, and the thought of three soft, squishy kittens for my daughters to love and grow up with made me happy.

"Yes! Three kittens for three little girls. It's meant to be."

"I'll be right back." Jeff left to rescue the cold and hungry kittens.

Instantly, the girls fell in love with the three white kittens. Jaena named her kitten Snowball. Jo chose Snowflake. And three-year-old Jessica, who couldn't pronounce the letter "s," called her kitten Snow White, which came out as "No White."

No White's name proved to be prophetic. Two weeks later, the tiny kitten shed her beautiful white fur. She looked more like a rat than a cat. I rushed her to the vet's office, where he checked her thoroughly.

"She's a healthy little thing. No ringworm, and nothing seems wrong with her at all. When did you adopt her?" the vet said, handing Snow White back to me.

"Two weeks ago. We found her and her brothers abandoned and starving on a frigid night."

"Well, that explains it. You can tell what has happened in a cat's life by its fur. Snow White's fur loss is a trauma response. Her fur will grow back now that she's found a good home."

Over the next few weeks, Snow White's fur grew long and gray, not a speck of white anywhere. She was indeed No White.

We all need rescuing. "Savior" is one name for God. He delivers us from danger and death and gives us a safe, love-filled home.

Lord, we cannot rescue ourselves. Thank you for your loving kindness, which saved us.

Share how God rescued you.

—Beth

49. GERMAN HOSPITALITY

Practice hospitality.

(Romans 12:13)

A wunderbar (wonderful) experience awaited my husband and me when we visited our high school exchange daughter, Lisa, at her home in Germany.

Our weeklong stay with her immediate family—father Manfred, mom Karina, and younger brother Jonas—was such a delight. They surprised us with unlimited amounts of delicious German food and breathtaking scenic excursions through eastern Germany, the Czech Republic, and western Poland. A memorable afternoon featured a river cruise where we viewed lush, terraced hillsides of crops and vineyards. No day was complete without stopping for Manfred's favorite dessert, "Eis" (ice cream).

Another joyful blessing was spending time with Lisa's maternal grandparents, Opa and Oma, whose next-door home constantly hummed with various animated sounds. We often awoke in the mornings to industrious Opa working in his garden. Our breakfast table featured fresh blueberries, gherkins (pickles), and tomatoes.

Afternoons we'd find Opa, a master carpenter, in his "man cave," fashioning ingenious wood or metal creations. Terry, who doesn't speak German, talked to Opa while Katahdin sheep bleated in the background. Smiles and mutual respect developed as these two farmers talked.

Oma's gift was hospitality. Her exuberant embraces, tasty treats, and knitted socks were her trademarks. She and Opa's infectious energy led us to dub them "party animals." One late night, we returned from touring to find their yard full of cars. Their party room nearly overflowed, and Oma led singing while playing the accordion.

Our week's finale found us at Opa's hand-constructed wood cabin in the hills behind their property. Lisa's extended family set out a smorgasbord of unforgettable food on the table Opa had crafted. As German conversation swirled around us, Terry and I marveled at how our new family readily accepted us.

Paul says, "For we were all baptized by one Spirit so as to form one body—whether Jews or Gentiles, slave or free—and we were all given the one Spirit to drink" (1 Corinthians 12:13).

Lord, what encompassing love you show us. Help us to live by your example.

How can you model Christ's hospitality today?

—Susan

50. FREEZING CORN

> But in fact God has placed the parts in the body, every one of them, just as he wanted them to be. If they were all one part, where would the body be? As it is, there are many parts, but one body ... Now you are the body of Christ, and each one of you is a part of it.
>
> (1 Corinthians 12:18–20, 27)

"Girls, come here. Let me teach you how to shuck corn."

Jeff waited for the girls to encircle him at the back of our minivan, a back filled with hundreds of ears of corn.

"First, you grab half of the husks, making sure you grab half the silks also. Then you pull down toward the bottom of the ear. Don't worry about pulling the husks off. Just let them dangle there. Then pull the other half of the husks and silk down. Last, you break all the husks off at once. See, no silk."

I watched as Jaena and Jo struggled until they figured out the method and began helping their dad. Jessica tried, but her little arms just didn't have enough muscle. Soon she was back to pulling one strand at a time. Thankfully, she took much longer to finish her ears because I had difficulty removing all the silk.

Yet, I was thankful for the girl's help. With them helping, the hot, messy chore took considerably less time than planned.

Inside the air-conditioned kitchen, Rita and I took over the next phase of the process, preparing the corn for the freezer. Soon my back ached, and my hands felt frozen from standing over a sink of cold water, washing each ear for Rita to cut off the kernels. All afternoon, we washed, cut, bagged, and microwaved corn. By the end of the day, we filled the freezer with over one hundred quarts of corn. We would enjoy delicious winter meals.

My mom said, "Many hands make light work."

That day, our family was a picture of Christ's body, the church. We each had a task and performed to the best of our abilities. The result was many meals of sweet corn.

Lord, may our family, and those who work at our farm, work as a team—the way you intended.

What is your part in the body of Christ in the functioning of your farm? How can you make the farm a healthier body today?

—Beth

51. EARTHLY ANGELS

> For he will command his angels concerning you to guard you in all your ways.
>
> (Psalm 91:11)

Our family always prays for traveling safety and a memorable trip as we leave our driveway for our destination. I personally add in a flash prayer that our truck or car is in good running condition.

As Terry and I hit I-70 westbound for the Junior National Hereford Expo in Kansas City, Missouri, and had traveled past Effingham, Illinois, our truck lost "umph," and we moved to the shoulder. Our truck and livestock trailer, holding four Herefords, cruised the shoulder for nearly ten miles. I immediately went into prayer mode and asked the Lord to send his angels to protect us.

Send us angels, he did. Eventually, we pulled into a Stuckey's and parked in the shade. A woman, parked next to us with an empty livestock trailer, offered to haul our cattle to the county fairgrounds a few miles away if we desired. As Terry worked under the truck hood, more than a dozen people stopped and offered to help. One couple offered to take Terry back to Effingham to an auto parts store. The husband worked for Effingham Equity and generously used his corporate discount for our parts and antifreeze.

We had planned to have dinner with Terry's crazy college roommate, who lived near St. Louis, but he and his wife "happened" to be traveling home from a trip to Indianapolis. They pulled into Stuckey's parking lot ten minutes after Terry left. They stayed with me, and we shared a quick meal with much laughter before we hit the road with a repaired truck.

A most memorable part of the trip was me accidentally dropping Terry's ancient cell phone into a Stuckey's restroom commode. I scared everyone in the restroom with my yelling as I fished out the phone. Three years of nagging, a truck breakdown, and a drop in a toilet finally forced Terry to buy a smartphone.

Thank you, Lord, for reminding us to pray at the start of the trip, surrounding us with earthly angels and friends, and consistently placing your protective shield around us.

When has the Lord sent an earthly angel to help you? Thank him for his provision.

—Susan

52. THE DRIVE-BY MOTHER-IN-LAW

> The Lord watches over you—the Lord is your shade at your right hand.
>
> (Psalm 121:5)

"Your mom's here, Jeff."

I watched Rita's gray van pull into our circular driveway.

"Are you sure? I don't see her."

My husband's back was to me as he scanned the driveway.

"Never mind. I see her heading down the road."

Why does she do that? It's kind of creepy.

At first, I resented Rita's drive-bys, feeling they were intrusive. I wanted to know the reason for these visits, which never actually became visits. After another drive-by incident, I voiced my complaint.

"Why does she do that? Is she checking up on me? Is she checking to see how high my weeds are?"

I felt her silent judgment as I looked at my overgrown flower beds.

"She's just being neighborly, checking to make sure all is well here, that there've been no break-ins or accidents."

I breathed a sigh of relief at Jeff's response and began

looking forward to seeing Rita on her neighborhood watch.

Many years later, when Rita and I were discussing our flowerbed, she told me she loved driving through our driveway in the spring to watch the progress of the peony, iris, lily, and Hosta perennials that bordered our home. She was not only watching over us but also enjoying the beauty my years of gardening labor had produced. She wasn't judging; she was admiring.

God does the same. He watches over us. But he also enjoys watching us grow and bloom into his image.

Lord, thank you for your watchful eye. May my life bring you joy and pleasure.

List times when you have been aware of God watching over you. Then list some ways you are growing as a Christian.

—Beth

53. WEDDING AT THE FARM

> And the Lord's servant must not be quarrelsome but must be kind to everyone, able to teach, not resentful.
>
> (2 Timothy 2:24)

Have you ever watched the movie *The Wedding Planner*? Actress Jennifer Lopez stars as a high-end wedding planner in San Francisco. I now appreciate why such a position makes big bucks. Every dollar is well earned.

While immersed in planning Lillian's September 2020 wedding, our family learned a few things. First, my daughter and I both like to be in control. Second, I'm a traditionalist, while Lillian is a Pinterest fanatic. I'm all about booking the church, the reception site, caterer, baker, florist—and, of course, shopping for *the* dress and accessories. Lillian scoured hundreds of pins she'd selected over the years while dating her husband, Kegan. For those uneducated on Pinterest (don't worry, I was), the pins are ideas for everything wedding—and I mean everything.

I cast my traditionalism aside. When COVID-19 struck, the church wedding became a farm wedding. My prayer warrior breastplate quickly became armed. Prayers centered on the wedding day going smoothly, asking for low humidity and clear skies and securing a borrowed sound system and microphone that worked. Countless flare prayers were catapulted to heaven as the wedding day approached.

The north side of our home's lawn became the church. A handmade cross provided the focal point. Edison lights were strung over straw bales covered in beautiful family-made or borrowed quilts. A big white tent was set for a reception dinner featuring a 4-H hog roasted by family friends. Tables sported fall mums and candles.

My worries were for naught. The Lord provided a perfect wedding day. Several of my best friends came from all over the country to be my buffers, helping wherever needed that week. As I walked out of the house in my mother-of-the-bride finery and gazed at preparations, I felt the Lord stop me and whisper clearly, "This has been a Holy-Spirit powered week." The Lord's peace flowed through me.

Eternally gracious Lord, I am overcome with your provision, tenderness, and voice. You never cease to amaze me. Amen.

What do you have an iron grip on right now? Release it and cover it with prayer.

—Susan

54. GREEN THUMB, BROWN THUMB

> You care for the land and water it; you enrich it abundantly. The streams of God are filled with water to provide the people with grain, for so you have ordained it. You drench its furrows and level its ridges; you soften it with showers and bless its crops. You crown the year with your bounty, and your carts overflow with abundance.
>
> (Psalms 65:9–11)

"Come see my African violet starts."

Dad led me to his kitchen window, where several Dixie cups lined the sill. Each cup contained a single leaf where tiny roots had sprouted, reaching down into the water in the cups.

"Dad, you and your green thumb!"

"Next time you come, I should have them planted and ready for you to take a couple home."

"Thanks. These new varieties you found are gorgeous."

I hope I don't kill them. I looked down at my hands. If thumbs actually got their coloring from one's ability to grow plants, mine would have a more brownish tint than green. As much as I love plants, indoor and out, I'm not the best plant caretaker. I forget to water them and treat all plants like cacti.

As a teenager, I watched the episode of *Little House on the Prairie* when Laura carried water to her drought-stricken garden. I remember thinking I'd never have the stamina or willpower to care for a garden like that. I'm more of the let's-plant-it-and-let-God-water-it type of gardener. My garden reflects that principle.

I'm so glad God doesn't treat us like that. He didn't create us and then say, "You're on your own now." No, God is the master gardener, and we flourish when we allow him to care for us.

Lord, thank you for caring for your creation. Thank you for tending to and providing for my family and me.

How do you see God caring for you and those you love today?

—Beth

GOODNESS

But the fruit of the Spirit is love, joy, peace, forbearance, kindness, goodness, faithfulness, gentleness and self-control. Against such things there is no law.

—Galatians 5:22–23

55. GOD'S TIMING IS PERFECT

> Trust in the Lord with all your heart and lean not unto your own understanding. In all your ways submit to him, and he will make your paths straight.
>
> (Proverbs 3:5–6)

Terry had always hoped to have a hog facility on his farm. When we married, we made his desire a matter of prayer. Four years into our marriage, while living a few miles from the farm, Terry burst into the house with news.

"Honeybear, a local businessman who owns the hog farm adjacent to the home farm wants to sell! He's giving us the first chance to buy it."

Tears of excitement filled Terry's sparkling blue eyes. Not only did we have the rental facility, but this new endeavor also included several barns and an old farmhouse. The farm also backed up to the one hundred acres of crop ground Terry and his dad had purchased when Terry graduated from college.

Terry, his dad, and the owner discussed the sale at length. The bank finally set up a meeting. The gathering included bank officers, the businessman, my in-laws, Terry, me, and Lillian, who was an infant at the time. While Terry and I signed the hog farm purchase agreement, my father-in-law, Dale, pulled out another paper from his briefcase.

"I'd like to share something I've discovered about the property's purchase agreement. Note the date when our family purchased the adjoining one hundred acres several years ago."

The businessman glanced at the date. Then, with a surprised look, he said, "Well, isn't that something."

The acreage purchase agreement had been signed nine years from the day we were buying the hog farm. Everyone in the room was awed by the revelation. Terry and I looked at each other, knowing it was more than just a coincidence. The purchase was a "Godwink" engineered by the Lord—an answer to Terry's desire to grow the farm. Most of all, it demonstrated the power of prayer and God's goodness.

Lord, we can be impatient as we anticipate answers to our prayers. You make us wait for just the right moments to unveil your blessings. Help us to trust your timing.

Are you waiting on an answer to a specific prayer today? Know God's answer is perfect.

—Susan

56. FIRST-TIME TRACTOR DRIVER

Never will I leave you; never will I forsake you.
> (Hebrews 13:5)

"Just push this button, and it'll start moving forward."

Jeff was giving me a quick lesson in tractor driving because he needed me to disk while he ran a quick errand.

"How do I stop when I get to the end of the row?"

"Don't worry about that. I'll be right back. If you reach the end of the row, turn and start the next row. I will be back before you need to stop." He jumped down and ran off.

Terror filled my body. I felt light-headed and wondered what would happen if I passed out. Would I keep going right over the ditch, across the road, and into the next field?

The tractor crept down the row in first gear. In the end, I managed to turn the monster around and start disking the next row. But my nerves were shot when Jeff came back a few minutes later.

"That's the last time I drive a tractor until you teach me how to stop it!" I stomped off, my boots flinging loose dirt behind me.

Have you ever been asked to do a job without having

the proper skills? Are you ever given a task without understanding everything you need to complete it? We don't always get all the answers we need in life. Parenting contains no owner's manual. There's no guidebook in decision-making. But God is good. He promises to be with us every step of the way. All we need to do is ask for his guidance.

Lord, help me remember you are with me when I feel overwhelmed and under-equipped.

Where do you need to ask God for directions? Trust that he is waiting to answer.

—Beth

57. UNEXPECTED GROCERIES

> For you were once darkness, but now you are light in the Lord. Live as children of light.
>
> (Ephesians 5:8–9)

Where were our next groceries going to come from? I had just finished paying bills, and, as usual, the paycheck didn't stretch far enough. As wean-to-finish hog producers in 1998, we were in the middle of the country's frightening economic farm downturn. Average hog prices had plummeted by $50 per hundredweight.

I knew Terry was even more frustrated than I was. Believing God gave him the desire to have a hog operation—along with his Polled Hereford cattle herd and crops—he wanted to honor the Lord's provision. Animal health was often an issue with weaners. One day, Terry came into the house looking dejected.

"Honey, we've had another infection outbreak in the weaner barns."

"How bad is it?" I asked, afraid of his answer.

"We've lost another six, and more are sick," he replied. "I'm going to have to take them to Purdue for diagnosis."

Not the news we needed. With an already crunched daily schedule, Terry often had to load the sick pigs into the livestock trailer for trips to Purdue University's Large

Animal Clinic for observation, tests, and vaccines. That meant more worry about animal death, expense, and large bills.

One day, my in-laws, Dale and Betty Jo, walked into our kitchen with bags of groceries. I was overwhelmed and broke into tears.

"Susie, we know this is a difficult time," Betty Jo said. "We thought these groceries would help for a while." They continued to bring groceries for a few months.

This was a lesson in humility for me. But, more importantly, I saw a fruit of the Holy Spirit—goodness—lived out in front of me.

Gracious Lord, thank you for in-laws who live out your Word daily. In your name, amen.

Look for ways to be Jesus's hands and feet today.

—Susan

58. AH, THE SMELL OF MONEY

> For we are to God the pleasing aroma of Christ among those who are being saved and those who are perishing. To the one we are an aroma that brings death; to the other, an aroma that brings life. And who is equal to such a task?
>
> (2 Corinthians 2:15–16)

"Ah, the smell of money."

My grandpa always said those words when he caught a strong whiff of pigs. *How could anyone like the smell of hogs?* I thought he was crazy when I was a kid. Yet, the tang of swine marked our arrival at my grandparent's farm, a place I loved, despite its stink.

But after living on a farm for many years, I've come to appreciate the smell. Notice I did not say enjoy or like or, heaven forbid, love the scent. Hogs smell like manure to me. But I do realize the benefits—like bacon, ham, and pulled pork sandwiches.

How ironic that we lived across the road from a large hog operation for twenty-six years. Even though we weren't raising that pork, we still got to enjoy its pre-barbecue fragrance. Some days, the smell overwhelmed my delicate city-girl constitution, and I ran for the house, slamming any open window shut. But on other days, I got only a hint of the scent, and I was gently reminded of my hardworking, pig-loving grandpa.

As Christians, we are meant to smell like Christ to the world. We are called to attract others to him through our aroma that is lived out in our actions and speech. Do we give off the scent of our Savior?

Lord, may all I do and say today cause those I contact long to know you more.

What can you do today to be the fragrance of Christ?

—Beth

59. HEED THE NUDGING

God is our refuge and strength, a very present help in trouble.

(Psalm 46:1)

Falling asleep on the couch or in the recliner, waiting for the late news, is the norm for Terry and me. One night we awoke at 11:30 p.m., and, as we groped our way through the darkened house toward our bedroom, I felt led to look out toward the barn lot. I saw two beams of light illuminating the livestock trailer sitting next to one of the barns.

"Terry, is the kitchen sink light reflecting brightly in the barn lot?"

He paused to consider my question, then exclaimed an emphatic "No!" as he threw on old tennis shoes, grabbed his flashlight, and dashed out of the house.

I watched him run around the corner of the farm shop. A few moments later, the bright lights disappeared. Terry ran in and out of the shop before walking into the house a few minutes later. In the dim kitchen light, I saw a look of alarm in his eyes.

"Are you alright? What happened?" My worry mounted.

"The two-wheel drive tractor was on fire."

Terry explained that the intense heat had melted the air conditioner hoses and fried the electrical wires on the motor. Together, those issues shorted out the electrical system and tripped the lights. Coincidence that I noticed the light? I think not.

That day, Terry and his helper had emptied the machinery shed of all equipment to prepare for planting season. They left the tractor and planter out to prep the following day. Had those pieces of equipment been inside, we would have never seen the lights or the fire until it was too late.

Instantly my eyes teared up as I realized God had turned those lights on to warn us something was wrong.

Life on the farm is never dull. But God, our protector, is always close, reminding us of our total dependence on him from planting through harvest.

Precious Lord, thank you for your arms of protection constantly surrounding us.

It should not take a crisis to entrust everything to our Lord. Give it to God today.

—Susan

60. THE ANHYDROUS THIEF

> A good man brings good things out of the good stored up in his heart, and an evil man brings evil things out of the evil stored up in his heart. For the mouth speaks what the heart is full of.
>
> (Luke 6:45)

The hose attached to the anhydrous ammonia tank flipped around in the air like a runway firehose.

"Dad, I think someone just tried to steal anhydrous!" Jeff yelled to his dad through the tractor's radio speaker.

"You're right. They just passed me."

Jeff's father, one field over, had watched a white car filled with deadly fumes pass him.

"I'm at the end of the row. I'll go shut the valve off."

Jeff grabbed his heavy leather work gloves from the dash and pulled a bandanna over his mouth and nose.

"Be careful!"

Jumping down from the tractor, Jeff ran toward the tank, sitting just feet from the road. Before getting too close, he inhaled deeply, plugged his nose as he ran, and twisted shut the valve. Despite all his efforts, Jeff's eyes stung, his chest hurt, and he struggled to breathe.

Even though the pilfered tank had been nearly empty, the fumes still damaged Jeff's lungs. For days, he felt as if he had a chest cold. A little bit of the dangerous chemical is enough to harm a person.

Likewise, a small amount of bitterness, envy, or anger can cause us pain. And our relationships suffer if those negative emotions are uncorked on those we love. We must work through hurt feelings, forgive each other, and fill our emotional tanks and hearts with God's goodness.

Lord, may our tanks be filled with your Spirit so that only love, joy, peace, patience, kindness, goodness, and self-control spill out.

Take some time today to fill your tank with the Word of God.

—Beth

61. WATCH WHAT YOU PRAY FOR

My grace is sufficient for you, for my power is made perfect in weakness.

(2 Corinthians 12:9)

I anticipated Christmas. On December 14, 2010, we loaded our last semi-load of hogs, and every hog barn was finally empty. After twenty years of stress and chaotic schedules, we were out of the hog business. Within a few days, I asked Terry, "Can we go to my parents' house for Christmas? It's been several years since we've spent the holidays with them."

Terry responded quickly. "Yes. Let's pack and surprise the girls by picking them up at school."

After a quick call to my parents in Florida, we were on the road. Spending a week eating at our favorite seafood restaurants, sunning on the beach, playing shuffleboard at their retirement park, and enjoying outdoor concerts on the village green seemed like heaven.

While I visited with Mom and Dad on their lanai Christmas Eve morning, my phone rang.

"Hi, Sara!"

"Oh my gosh. You don't know," Sara said, tears choking her voice.

"Know what?" I asked.

"You have a huge fire burning at your farm," she replied.

Within minutes, Terry received multiple calls with the news. The four-alarm fire consumed our implement shed and machinery shop. We lost three-quarters of our farm equipment, including three generations of tools. The fire was still smoldering when we arrived home thirty-six hours later.

My 2010 word for the year was *grace*. I had asked the Lord to help me better understand his grace. On the day of the fire, grace was the wind blowing from the east instead of the west, saving our home, which was only thirty feet from the shop. Grace saved us from seeing the desecration firsthand. Grace gave us a fabulous week with my parents. God's grace embodied itself in our friends and family who pitched in at a dire time. Grace wrapped us in the Lord's protection as we drove home through a blizzard.

Precious Lord, thank you for showing us that your grace strengthens and covers us no matter where we are. In Jesus's name, amen.

Consider how the Lord manifests his grace in your life.

—Susan

62. A TEXAS OLIVE GROVE

Then God said, 'Let the land produce vegetation: seed-bearing plants and trees on the land that bear fruit with seed in it, according to their various kinds.' And it was so. The land produced vegetation: plants bearing seed according to their kinds and trees bearing fruit with seed in it according to their kinds. And God saw that it was good.

(Genesis 1:11–12)

"Olive trees need a particular climate to grow, yet in the right location, they're like weeds that refuse to die. You cut them down, but they will come right back up."

I could tell the arborist enjoyed his work and sharing the uniqueness of olive trees. He explained how he cared for the grove. My friends and I followed him along the rows of shrub-like trees in the dry Texas heat, soaking up all his knowledge.

Once inside the stone building, we tasted flavored oils and toured the pressing room, where the owner explained the process of making oil and its many benefits.

Olive oil is rich in compounds that help lower the risk of Alzheimer's, dementia, and cognitive decline. The oil contains antioxidants that protect against free radicals that can cause cancer, diabetes, and inflammation. God's creation is "very good."

Yet, the loveliest discovery for me was that olive trees live for hundreds of years. Jerusalem has olive trees that were there when Jesus was alive. You can walk through an Israeli olive grove and touch a tree that Jesus may have sat under. Amazing!

I left the olive grove that day, reminded of the blessing of tending God's creation.

Lord, help me to see my farm through your eyes, the eyes of the Creator.

As you work today, thank God for the privilege of caring for his creation, the land, and animals.

—Beth

63. NEVER SAY NEVER

> I will sing of the LORD's great love forever; with my mouth I will make your faithfulness known through all generations.
>
> (Psalm 89:1)

Riding a horse for the first time when I was nine was scary but exhilarating. Equally terrifying was ending up in an oxygen tent in the hospital immediately after riding. Why? I was allergic to animal dander.

A few weeks later, my mom took me to my first allergist appointment with a saint of a man, Dr. Marvel. Yes, that was his name.

"Mrs. Krauch, Susie needs allergy tests right away. The horse episode was the trigger for asthma."

Four hours of testing revealed I was allergic to animal dander and hay and straw, dust mites, mold and mildew, ragweed, and pollen. Dr. Marvel's diagnosis was serious.

"Susie must start weekly allergy shots and will be on them for several years. The asthma attack happened on a farm. She must never go to a farm again or marry a farmer."

Mom and Dad bought an air purifier for my bedroom, installed central air conditioning in our home, and took me for my shots—followed by cathartic ice cream cones.

They drilled into me that I was to go nowhere near a farm for fear of another asthma attack.

The Lord has a tremendous sense of humor. Years later, while I helped organize my tenth high school reunion, my dear friend, DeeDee, set me up on a blind date with a guy named Terry, who was a farmer. He proposed four months after our first date, and eight months later, we married.

Precious Lord, when we say never, you frequently ask, "Why not?" Thank you so much.

Never is a very long time. What blessings await you if you put fear away?

—Susan

64. A STINKY SITUATION

The Lord is good, a refuge in times of trouble. He cares for those who trust in him.

(Nahum 1:7)

When our girls were little, my husband and I converted an old chicken coop into a playhouse. First, Jeff brought the backhoe down and moved the sturdy but dirty structure nearer to our house. I swept dust, dirt, and cobwebs from the inside and painted the exterior white, transforming the coop into a darling little playhouse.

The girls and I hauled out the kitchen play set and child-sized table from our crowded tiny home and filled the playhouse with the necessary items to complete it. The girls spent hours playing house, making meals for each other and their dolls.

"Mom, something smells really bad out there," Jaena screamed as she ran to the house for safety.

I stuck my head out the back door, and a strong skunk odor met me.

"Girls, come inside. Hurry!" I rushed the other two girls inside before the angry skunk sprayed them. Then I yelled to Jeff, "There's a skunk outside. Come quick."

We discovered a momma skunk and several tiny babies had taken up residence under our lovely playhouse.

We banned the girls from playing outside until the stinky family was rehomed far away. Unfortunately, the playhouse was off limits for quite a while.

We each come to a moment when we realize we have the odor of sin around and on us and need forgiveness. Thankfully, when we recognize our sinfulness, God stands ready to wash us clean, giving us the scent of him: sweet, clean, and holy. And his cleansing is immediate and complete, leaving no residue of sin.

Lord, thank you for forgiving us of our sins and making us clean and pure.

What is the scent of your life? Do you need Christ's cleansing?

—Beth

FAITHFULNESS

But the fruit of the Spirit is love, joy, peace, forbearance, kindness, goodness, faithfulness, gentleness and self-control. Against such things there is no law.

—Galatians 5:22–23

65. BEGOTTEN HEREFORDS

He will be great and be called the Son of the Most High. The Lord God will give him the throne of his father David, and he will reign over Jacob's descendants forever; his kingdom will never end.

(Luke 1:32–33)

When reading the Old Testament, have you ever wondered why there are so many "begats?"

For many years, I've skipped over or ignored that annoying word because I found it boring. But, honestly, what is the significance of the long line of strange-named men who all seem to be related to one another?

Webster's dictionary defines begat as "to procreate as the father: sire." The Bible contains countless fathers who were long-standing patriarchs in their families.

One day, my daughter Hayley pointed out that our Hereford cattle pedigrees resemble the lineages cited in the Bible. In addition, our Polled Hereford cattle's registrations with the American Hereford Association specifically detail the dams and sires of our herd. The recording of such information reflects the heritage and legacy of our cattle operation and thousands of other producers in the US.

Terry, Hayley, and I were once privileged to visit Herefordshire, England, and tour Hereford operations.

One farm, The Haven at Dilwyn, Hereford, is the oldest Hereford operation in the world and is operated by its fifth generation, the Edward Lewis family. They proudly display their Hereford and family's concurrent genealogy in a mounted timeline in their farm's conference room. We were thrilled to discover our Herefords are connected to their ancestors, who came from England in the late 1800s.

The Word was the first example of such a tradition. We can read, study, and learn the Lord's intentional creation of so many of our forebears through God-breathed Scripture. The lives and stories of Joseph and David are prime testimonies of faith legacies.

Why is genealogy so important? Through Christ, we are begotten spiritually from the house of David, just as Jesus, our Savior, was of David's lineage. We are all children of God our Father and brothers and sisters of Jesus.

Appreciating our farm's cattle lineage is important. But, standing in awe of our biblical birthright to the Lord of Lords and the King of Kings surpasses any begat hang up I could ever have. I'm in awe of being begotten by my risen Savior.

Thank you, Lord, for showing me the value of a seemingly insignificant word in Scripture.

Reflect today on your family heritage. What legacy will you leave for those who follow you?

—Susan

66. WHAT DOES A FARMER DO?

I seek you with all my heart; do not let me stray from your commands. I have hidden your word in my heart that I might not sin against you.

(Psalm 119:10-11)

One fine spring day, I hauled a suitcase full of food items to a local school to give an agricultural classroom presentation.

After setting up my supplies (we were making pizzas to help kids understand where different types of food come from), the teacher gathered the students onto the rug around me.

"What does a farmer do?"

I thought an opening question would help me gauge the knowledge of the urban third graders.

"He drives a tractor," a boy shouted.

"They plant corn and feed cows."

Quickly, the students fired answers back at me.

These were the typical answers. All correct. Then I saw a boy in a red shirt near the back raise his hand, and I called on him.

"They keep the fox out of the chicken house." He beamed with pride.

Momentarily, I was caught off guard, but then I

remembered the Disney movie my girls loved to watch, *The Fox and the Hound*. I knew this young boy had learned all about the farm from watching the cute but outdated movie.

I spent the next hour teaching the class what ingredients go into a pizza and where those products come from—but more importantly, that men and women are farmers. Some farmers do have chickens, but others have cows, and cows give us the final pizza topping, cheese. I'm glad I could expand and correct the boy in the red shirt's farming knowledge.

Do we know who God is and how he wants us to live? Or are our answers based on incomplete or incorrect knowledge? In God's goodness, he gave us the Bible, a reference, to correct wrong thinking or ignorance.

Lord, help me point others to you through my knowledge of your Word.

Pick a Bible verse and hide the words in your heart by memorizing them.

—Beth

67. ROOTED IN FARMING

> I planted the seed, Apollos watered it, but God made it grow ... For we are co-workers in God's service; you are God's field, God's building.
>
> (1 Corinthians 3:6, 9)

Charles E. Kellogg, a recognized soil scientist, once said, "As a farmer, man himself became closely attached to the landscape, firmly rooted to the soil that supported him. At times the soil seemed bountiful and kindly and again stubborn and unfriendly, but it was always a challenge to man's cunning."

I don't believe I've ever encountered a profession where someone is more firmly rooted in it than farming. The soil—the land—can be so immeasurably prolific, yet months later be just as unforgiving. A farmer and their land are like the strongest magnet in the world. Nothing, except unforeseen forces, can break the bond.

Farming takes back-breaking, budget-shifting, stress-inducing passion—entailing a war of the will at times. Yet farmers come back for more every day, month, year, and season. Chris Dearden, a producer in Napa, California, shared in *The Furrow*, "This cyclical nature of our business is really a great thing. It's a renewal ... When we are in the thick of it, I don't have time to think about why I love it."

Experiencing a renewal can happen at any moment. Smelling freshly mown hay. Watching the birth of a calf. Loading the planter for a final pass. Sharing a meal in the field. Taking a moment on bended knee to offer thanks to the Lord.

Isaiah 58:11 sums up how being rooted and depending on the Lord should be our first passion: "The Lord will guide you always; he will satisfy your needs in a sun scorched land and will strengthen your frame. You will be like a well-watered garden, like a spring whose waters never fail."

God, thank you for the privilege of being stewards of your creation.

Examine your heart. Is it time for a much-needed renewal?

—Susan

68. FAULTY EQUIPMENT

Rise up and help us; rescue us because of your unfailing love.

(Psalm 44:26)

One day Jeff asked Jo, our thirteen-year-old daughter, to drive an old van from the field across the road to the farm. Not a difficult job ... typically. But in this case, the old gray van's brakes were somewhat less than reliable. To get them to work, Jo would need to begin braking long before braking in a typical vehicle. Such is life on the farm. We run our vehicles to death and then park them in the automotive graveyard down the lane.

Jo hopped in the dust-covered van and drove across the field and onto the road. But when she pushed on the brakes to turn into the driveway, the brakes chose, at that moment, to quit working. The van kept right on moving. The van slowed at its own pace, not with the quickness demanded by the teenaged foot punching the pedal to the floor.

Uncle Jason ran down the drive, arriving just as the van came to a stop on a guidewire and moments away from taking down an electric pole. Stunned, Jo put the van in park and stumbled out. She ran to my car, letting her uncle finish the task.

What teenager doesn't get excited by driving? Are there times when we get excited about opportunities beyond our abilities or knowledge? Have you ever failed from lack of experience, improper tools, or faulty thinking? Thankfully, like Uncle Jason, we have a God who runs to our rescue in our time of need.

Lord, thank you for rescuing us when we are unprepared, ill-equipped, or foolish. Equip us for the task ahead.

Ask God for his guidance and protection as you work today.

—Beth

69. FLICKERING LIGHTS

> Surely he will save you from the fowler's snare and from the deadly pestilence. He will cover you with his feathers, and under his wings you will find refuge; his faithfulness will be your shield and rampart.
>
> (Psalm 91:3-4)

"Why are the lights flickering," I asked Terry, who watched television.

"I don't know, but I'll check the electrical box in the basement."

This wasn't the first time we had intermittent lighting problems. I knew it wasn't unusual for our old circa 1930s farmhouse to have aging electrical lines. I also knew repairs or renovation on the house was far down on the list behind farm expenses.

Terry returned from the basement and said some wires had arced, causing a short.

"I will need to do some minor rewiring on the box."

"I hope it will be sooner rather than later. This situation makes me nervous," I said with fear already building.

Several days later, the rewiring hadn't been done, and the lights flickered again. Terry was busy with the farm, so I called our favorite electrician, Joe. When he arrived, he headed for the basement, knowing where to look. Soon, I heard, "Susan, you'll want to see this."

As I reached the bottom of the stairs, I found Joe with the electrical box open and a concerned expression on his face.

"This is why your lights have been flickering again."

The entire inside of the big box was black. Singed. I immediately crumbled, knowing we had escaped a fire. The Lord had sent warnings through the spotty lighting. His love and faithfulness had protected us.

How often do I put off important tasks? Does the Lord protect me from accident or calamity? Are my priorities more important than where the Holy Spirit is leading me? I needed to come before the One who knows what is best for all.

Father God, you are our great protector. We need your guardianship and blanket of security. Help us to put you first always. Amen.

How can you better protect your family today? Make a list and prioritize it.

—Susan

70. VEGAS

> Therefore I tell you, do not worry about your life, what you will eat or drink; or about your body, what you will wear. Is not life more than food, and the body more than clothes? Look at the birds of the air; they do not sow or reap or store away in barns, and yet your heavenly Father feeds them. Are you not much more valuable than they? ... Therefore do not worry about tomorrow, for tomorrow will worry about itself. Each day has enough trouble of its own.
>
> (Matthew 6:25–26, 34)

"When we get to Vegas, what shows do you want to see? Blue Man Group?" our friend asked his wife as they planned their summer vacation.

"Oh, we saw them in Chicago. You will like them," another friend chimed in.

This was a passing conversation during an evening with friends. But I couldn't get the idea out of my head. Vacations were not something we regularly took, and when we did, we usually visited family. I wondered what Jeff thought about Vegas as a vacation destination. I liked the idea of seeing some of the shows our friends had pondered over attending.

Later, in the car, I asked Jeff, "Would you ever want to go to Vegas?"

"No. Every day is a gamble when you're a farmer. Either the weather's too hot or too cold. The ground is too dry or too wet. One year, weeds are a problem. The next, bugs invade. Then the prices or the yields are too low. Or we get a good price, but then fertilizer costs go up. I have enough to worry about here at home. I have no desire to take any more risks by going to Vegas."

In the farming profession, farming can seem like gambling, and worry can be our constant companion if allowed. Jesus wants us to remember our value. He watches over and loves his creation. Me, you, and the land.

Lord, help us keep worry far from our minds. When we are tempted to concentrate on our troubles, remind us that you take care of us.

When tempted to worry today, remember God will take care of you.

—Beth

71. CALLED TO PRAY

"Because he loves me," says the Lord, "I will rescue him;
I will protect him, for he acknowledges my name."
(Psalm 91:14)

The cold November morning began with a knock on our dining room door at eight o'clock. Our farm helper, obviously stressed, told me this was his last day working for us. As he left, I felt an urgency to find Terry.

I found him agitated and burdened in our rental hog facility's feed room. I told him I'd be home that afternoon and began to drive away when a clear voice spoke into my heart: "Pray for Terry."

Stunned at such an urgent charge, I immediately called my friend, Cissy, to pray with me and for Terry. I walked into the house several hours later.

"I have something to show you," Terry said as he pulled up the leg of his jeans. "This happened after you left this morning."

Terry had deep abrasions and contusions on his left leg and ankle and down the underside of his left arm. After I'd left, he headed for the cattle operation, loaded the silage feeder, and drove our Ford 801, "Little Henry," to the first cattle bunk. As the silage unloaded, Terry stepped onto the feeder's gearbox, and, in the blink of an eye, he was abruptly picked up, thrown down, and caught by his shredding work clothes moving into the feeder's PTO.

What can I do now? He'd thought. "All of a sudden, a warm peace flooded me, and the tractor died. As I regained my composure and realized where I was, I unwrapped myself and found my pocketknife. I got up, walked to the truck, and drove home to clean up."

When our doctor examined and X-rayed Terry five days later (yes, he's a farmer), he showed us from the tip of Terry's toe to the top of his leg where bones should have been broken. He was stunned that not even one bone had been chipped or his skin broken.

Was it a coincidence that the tractor died? Or that his skin, leg, or foot weren't broken? Why did the PTO stop? We believe a miracle happened that day. Prayer is powerful.

What a mighty God you are, Lord. Thank you for saving Terry and covering him with your ever-flowing grace and mercy.

Farming is a dangerous job. Meditate gratefully today on how the Lord has protected you from harm.

—Susan

72. CITY GIRL MOVES TO THE FARM

> In their hearts humans plan their course, but the Lord establishes their steps.
>
> (Proverbs 16:9)

It's a story as old as time. A city girl—well, a small-town girl—meets a country boy—well, a college boy heading to Detroit—and falls in love. Country boy takes small-town girl to suburban Detroit for three years and then moves her back to the family farm. How's that for cultural whiplash?

I never planned to live in the big city. But when I married a preacher, I never considered country life a possibility, even though I had fostered a sweet little daydream of living on a farm with some cats, a dog, a little pond with ducks, and a quiet place where I could sit outside and read a good book.

I was excited when we decided to leave Detroit for rural life, but farm life reality took me by surprise. Yes, I got a cute little farmhouse. No, the house did not have an indoor laundry room. Yes, I did have two cats, but they came with me from the city and were in as much culture shock as I was. Yes, there was a pond—across the road and behind the neighbor's house. There were no ducks, but lots of hogs.

And talk about that fresh country air. No afternoons in the shade unless I wanted to stink the rest of the day. Oh, and we lived just off a busy state road where semis drove sixty miles per hour past our front door. So I learned to listen to the engine's sound and distinguish between our trucks and those passing by.

Life often doesn't meet our expectations, especially when we've daydreamed about what that life could be. Sometimes, daydreaming hurts our acceptance of reality. But in my case, love conquered all, and over time, I grew to love living the farm life, the real farm life.

Lord, help us to trust you with our lives and let go of our expectations.

What are you daydreaming about? Can you hand over your dreams to God and accept the reality of your life?

—Beth

73. DO NOT WORRY

But seek first his kingdom and his righteousness, and all these things will be given to you as well. Therefore, do not worry about tomorrow, for tomorrow will worry about itself. Each day has enough trouble of its own.

(Matthew 6:33-34)

I couldn't stop worrying. My recent breast cancer diagnosis permeated my mental, physical, spiritual, and physical being for weeks. Through frequent rivers of tears, I constantly prayed, knowing my extended family and friends were also lifting my family and me in prayer.

One evening, as I stood at the kitchen sink washing dishes and trying to forget my body harbored the "C" word, Terry came in the door with his trademark beaming smile.

"Guess what, honeybear?"

"What?" I replied, feeling no emotion.

"I just found a new Case IH 4-wheel drive tractor for a good price. It's one of only nine of its kind available in the country!"

Knowing I should show joy for him was hard. Medical bills were racking up. Taking care of our two young daughters was wiping me out physically, especially since they had brought home head lice from school. Farm expenses always felt insurmountable. And now I wondered how we would absorb the tractor expense in the farm budget.

Wait, the Lord whispered. *Have I not provided for you? The cancer was caught at its earliest stage. Your friends and family help care for the girls. Terry needed the tractor, and I'm providing one. The bills will be paid.*

I was so consumed with myself that I missed the Lord's great faithfulness and mercies. He was providing for us in every direction. All I needed to do was lift my eyes away from the dirty mess in the sink and focus them on my Healer and our Provider.

Father God, forgive me for self-centeredness. Great are you, Lord, and worthy of praise.

Are you looking down instead of up? Trust that the Lord will raise you from the sinking sand.

—Susan

74. LEAVING THE FARM

> There is a time for everything, and a season for every activity under the heavens: a time to be born and a time to die, a time to plant and a time to uproot ... a time to weep and a time to laugh, a time to mourn and a time to dance ... a time to search and a time to give up, a time to keep and a time to throw away.
>
> (Ecclesiastes 3:1–2, 4, 6)

"How would you feel if we moved?" Jeff lowered his aching back onto the couch the evening after he finished harvest season.

I stared at him. *Is he joking? He doesn't look like he's joking.* I couldn't believe we were having this discussion. Jeff had been adamant that he would never retire, move, or leave the farm. But here he was asking the question I never imagined he'd ask. He loved farming, and I had settled into this home and farm life. I'd worked hard to put down roots, develop deep friendships, and find fulfilling work.

"Are you serious?"

"Yes, I can't do this anymore. I don't think my body can handle another season."

If leaving farming would be best, I was willing. "Yes. Let's try to find other jobs."

At that moment, a hidden door in our hearts was unlocked, the door leading to adventure. God set us on a new path when we opened the door and stepped through. I was offered a job where I could use my college degree, but we would need to move. Jeff found a job with a company allowing him to work from home and live anywhere.

Now, we are no longer farmers. We reconnected with my family, made new friends, found a new church, and said goodbye to family, friends, and our beloved home. A time of giving away possessions to make room for a new life. But most of all, we have learned to lean into God's faithfulness during the unknown.

Lord, thank you for your faithfulness to us when we follow you. Give us the strength to take the next step, trusting you will lead.

Where is God leading you?

—Beth

75. GREAT IS YOUR FAITHFULNESS

This is the confidence we have in approaching God: that if we ask anything according to his will, he hears us.

(1 John 5:14)

"Marrying my Lillian is proof prayers do come true."

Our son-in-law Kegan wrote and recited beautiful wedding vows to our daughter. His love for her poured out through his endearing words that are worthy of sharing in part.

"I asked the Lord for a farm girl who would cherish long talks of agriculture, ride for periods in the tractor, and above all else, be a cheerful Christian girl who would treat me and my daughter, Kaelynn, with the respect and love we deserved.

"One day, my grandpa gave me an *Indiana Prairie Farmer* magazine with a picture of two young ladies from a farm family that he knew very well. The picture included Lillian and her sister, Hayley. Grandpa told me that I should be talking to one of them. Little did I know I would call one of those girls my wife and the other a sister.

"Lilly, I am so blessed to have you in my life. It is crazy to think we have lived so closely to one another our whole lives, and we only first met a little over six years ago. You are just as beautiful on the inside as you are on the outside, which is a lot, in case you didn't know.

"I have been going through many hardships lately that I was almost positive would send you running in the other direction. But here you are, still loving me with all your heart, standing by my side, ready to tackle whatever comes our way.

"I just want you to know that no matter what, I'll be here for you whenever you need me. And even though I can't afford to give you the world, I can give you all of me, and that's what I promise I will do until the end of time."

The apostle Paul describes what love is and isn't. He says, "It always protects, always trusts, always hopes, always perseveres" (1 Corinthians 13:7).

Father of Love, thank you for Kegan's prayer and the answer you provided him.

Think of a prayer God answered for you. Then, share the story with someone today.

—Susan

GENTLENESS

But the fruit of the Spirit is love, joy, peace, forbearance, kindness, goodness, faithfulness, gentleness and self-control. Against such things there is no law.
—Galatians 5:22–23

76. MY CHICKEN HAS A BONE IN IT

> I meditate on your precepts and consider your ways. I delight in your decrees; I will not neglect your word.
> (Psalm 119:15–16)

The five of us—Jeff, our three girls, and me—sat for supper at the kitchen table. I was excited to try the new recipe I'd just made using chicken thighs. I was sure the family would love the dish which included family favorites: chicken and Ranch dressing. But, boy, was I wrong!

"Mom, my chicken has a bone in it!" Jessie stared down at her plate, thoroughly disgusted. I looked over at Jeff, waiting for him to back me up, but all I got was a nod and a shoulder shrug.

"Don't look at me. I don't like bones in my chicken either." He sat there, meticulously pulling chicken meat from the bone with his fork.

How could Jessie not realize chicken came with bones? And why wasn't Jeff more concerned?

I realized my daughter needed an anatomy lesson on chickens and probably other farm animals that find their way onto our plates. I was embarrassed that even though she lived on a farm, she didn't know this basic fact: animals have bones inside them.

But at least she knew chocolate milk didn't come from a brown cow. I hoped.

I think about my knowledge of the Bible, which sits on a bookshelf in my living room. I go to church every week. I know God. But am I missing important facts about my Creator? How much time do I spend getting to know him through his Word?

Lord, as I open my Bible today, help me understand you better through the words I read.

Spend a few minutes reading the Bible, asking God to reveal something new to you.

—Beth

77. EVEN COWS LIKE MUSIC

> Let us come before him with thanksgiving and extol him with music and song.
>
> (Psalm 95:2)

I've been told cattle enjoy calming background music in the barn. While this doesn't mesh with the loud music pulsating from stereo systems at cattle shows, I like to think our Polled Herefords are a gentle sort and appreciate the more refined tastes in music. When Terry works with our cattle, he tunes in to Christian music programming, but our daughters played country or pop hits when they prepped for the fair.

Has your livestock ever received a personal serenade?

We were thrilled when our girls had the option of playing in their fifth-grade school strings program. Lillian chose the cello, and Hayley selected the viola. They enjoyed playing concerts while on the phone with their faraway grandparents. The girls also played together at church.

One day, Hayley announced she wanted to play her viola outside. I thought that was a good idea. At least she would get her practice in for the day. Moments later, I looked out our dining room French doors and saw her standing near the show barn, serenading her and Lillian's cattle. The animals' heads were stuck through the open barn windows, their tongues were trying to lick her instrument, and others were bawling as she played. Their actions didn't daunt her. She continued to perform her school playlist.

My heart smiled, believing Hayley's music made the cattle happy, and the Lord's ears deemed her efforts praiseworthy to him.

Creator of music, I'm so grateful music appreciation runs in our family. Help us always to praise you.

What's your favorite hymn or uplifting song? Sing it loudly to the Lord.

—Susan

78. A STRONG OLD HOUSE

You also, like living stones, are being built into a spiritual house to be a holy priesthood, offering spiritual sacrifices acceptable to God through Jesus Christ. For in Scripture it says: 'See, I lay a stone in Zion, a chosen and precious cornerstone, and the one who trusts in him will never be put to shame.'

(1 Peter 2:5–7)

"Old country homes have their warts," so the saying goes. Small or nonexistent closets. Drafty old windows painted permanently shut. Squeaky floors that prevent sneaking to the fridge late at night. Oddities and inconveniences come with living in an old farmhouse, and our sweet century-old home had plenty of those flaws.

The downstairs ceilings reached eight feet, but upstairs, anyone over 5'11" had to duck or risk scraping their head. When we moved in, the laundry room was in a separate building, and the kitchen countertops were built low for the previous owner, who was short. I had grown used to living in a less-than-perfect house.

What I didn't expect was a positive attribute. When adding an addition, we decided to add siding so that the new and old parts of the house would match. During the process, I stepped outside to watch the workers turn our paint-peeling facade into a bright white home. Then, I walked over to where Jeff and our contractor huddled, deep in discussion.

"This house was so well built I could have ordered pre-cut siding from the factory. The measurements were that exact."

I looked at my home with new eyes. I've heard people say they don't make things as they used to, but that was the first time I'd experienced it. Our home had stood sound for over a century because the builders used a solid foundation with good materials and expert hands. Whoever built our house cared about making sure their work withstood the test of time.

These verses remind me I should care about my "spiritual house" like my home's original builder did his physical house. I must build on Jesus, the precious cornerstone. He is the one who helps me build my spiritual house strong and straight. When I allow the Master Builder to work, I can trust him to keep me steady when storms come.

Jesus, thank you for being the firm foundation for my spiritual house.

Are you trusting your life to Jesus, the chosen and precious cornerstone, or are you using your own strength to build your spiritual house?

—Beth

79. TOOLS OF THE TRADE

Your word is a lamp for my feet and a light on my path.
(Psalm 119:105)

Have you ever noticed that the dashboard of a farmer's truck resembles the contents of a woman's purse? A woman's purse usually carries what she considers the essentials (except for the kitchen sink). A truck's dashboard holds what a farmer uses daily, even hourly.

Purses and dashboards hold very practical items. Women whip out a trial-size tube of hand lotion, whereas men often reach for WD-40. If sticky fingers need cleaning up, women carry petite towelettes or hand sanitizer. Men's vehicles boast a roll of shop towels to scrub away grease and oil. Moms are known to have a few bandages for those boo-boos that need attention; men exercise their machismo and carry duct tape wherever they go.

Daily to-dos may be scribbled on a dusty envelope and thrown on the truck dashboard, but shopping lists are carefully noted on colored memo pads in the purse. Women dig in their satchels for chocolate-covered protein bars when they need an energy boost, while men grab a box of fuses off the dash.

Sun or sparks in your eyes? Don your colorful sunglasses or geeky safety goggles, depending on your choice. Women often enhance their identity by shopping using their wallets. Men count their tools.

As I sorted through the hodgepodge of things on our farm truck's dashboard, I felt it lacked something critical. Do our purses and dashboards boast the most indispensable item of all—the Bible? Perhaps our cell phones have Bible apps that we often use for encouragement and memorizing Scripture. We may tune our radios to our favorite praise program or minister's podcasts. But, do we take the Word with us—in our hearts and memory and everywhere we go?

Am I worried about carting around more, Lord, than taking you with me in body, mind, and soul?

Together, let's sort out our daily priorities and commit to carrying the Word in us.

—Susan

80. SWEEPING THE BIN

> Therefore, as God's chosen people, holy and dearly loved, clothe yourselves with compassion, kindness, humility, gentleness and patience. Bear with each other and forgive one another if any of you has a grievance against someone. Forgive as the Lord forgave you. And over all these virtues put on love, which binds them all together in perfect unity.
>
> (Colossians 3:12–14)

"I'll pay you to watch the sweep auger in the bin."

Sweet words for a teenager daughter to hear. Money was involved in this chore, an unusual opportunity. Jaena rushed to change into work clothes before her dad could change his mind.

An hour later, the back door flew open, and I heard huffing from two angry people.

"Five dollars? That's all?" Sweat dripped off her face as she rushed past me.

"She's lucky she got anything for sitting on a folding chair and doing nothing for an hour." My husband rolled his eyes.

This was a moment for me to practice gentleness—gentleness with an angry daughter and a frustrated husband. Unmet expectations had let each down. Jaena wanted the money she felt she deserved, and Jeff wanted an appreciative daughter.

"Let me talk to her." I smiled at Jeff and headed up the stairs to help smooth out hard feelings.

I think of times when I've fallen victim to unmet expectations. How well do I handle the disappointment? Do I harbor resentment or anger? Am I willing to search for common ground and work to resolve the miscommunication?

Reconciliation is always tricky but never more needed than when working with family.

Lord, guard our farms against little riffs that can fester into open hostility. Help us to be gentle with each other and quick to forgive.

How can you show gentleness to your family members today?

—Beth

81. CHICKENS AND A DOG NAMED SAM

Therefore, I tell you, whatever you ask for in prayer, believe that you have received it, and it will be yours.

(Mark 11:24)

Terry needed a new farm dog to herd cattle. His longtime companion, Captain, had passed away. So now, he hoped for an Australian shepherd or a blue heeler.

Terry's parents and I prayed for several months that God would send just the right dog. Then, one day, Terry's dad, Dale, pointed out a newspaper ad for a free blue heeler to go to a loving home. I called the dog's owners and discovered they only lived a short distance away. Their description of the dog made me think we'd found a perfect fit. Sam was very affectionate, a year old, well-trained, and gentle with people. Sound too good to be true?

Yes, Sam had one flaw. His owners lived next to a family who raised chickens in their backyard. Sam hated chickens. He would put his herding skills to work, rustle the chickens together, and then kill them. To preserve their relationship with their neighbor, Sam's family felt forced to find him another home.

Early in our relationship, Terry had emphatically said we would have no chickens on the farm. His dislike for chickens stemmed from a college spring break where he worked on an Arkansas chicken farm.

To introduce Terry to Sam, his folks and I kidnapped Terry from the field and put him into the back of my minivan. He fussed because he was losing valuable field time, but when we pulled into Sam's driveway, Terry bounded out of the van and headed right for the dog. Terry's beaming smile and Sam's wagging tail and slurps verified they'd make the perfect match.

Sam lived a long, chickenless life at Hayhurst Farms with his sidekick, Terry.

Thank you, Lord, that your matchmaking isn't only for humans. You bring us such joy through the animals you grace us with.

What are you praying for today? Believe you will receive it.

—Susan

82. FARMING IS NOT GARDENING

Listen and hear my voice; pay attention and hear what I say. When a farmer plows for planting, does he plow continually? Does he keep on breaking up and working the soil? When he has leveled the surface, does he not sow caraway and scatter cumin? Does he not plant wheat in its place, barley in its plot, and spelt in its field? His God instructs him and teaches him the right way.

(Isaiah 28:23–26)

I looked out over the expansive backyard. We had recently moved back to the farm and finally had a sunny yard large enough for a garden. And I knew right where I wanted to plant it. But, unfortunately, I didn't have a tiller. That didn't matter because Jeff had a plow. He could get the job done in two short rows. No problem. Or so I thought.

I don't know how I convinced him to plow up our lovely yard. Maybe young love blinded him. Perhaps he knew he couldn't convince me that using a plow wouldn't work. But, somehow, I sweet-talked him into the task.

In a matter of minutes, he had come and gone, leaving me with two long rows of lumpy soil. The huge, overturned hunks of hard clay sod were either grass side down or lying with the grass sideways. I planted cucumbers and melons in between where the blade cut into the yard, hoping they would cover and hide my ruined yard. I now know plowing is not tilling.

That first spring, I tried to be a gardener with a farmer's tools. What a failure! Not until I got an actual garden tiller and worked the soil properly did I raise an authentic vegetable garden.

I'm thankful God doesn't come into our lives and use a plow where tilling is needed. He doesn't get out a chainsaw and cut down everything when he prunes. Instead, he takes his pruning shears and makes gentle cuts, causing us to grow strong and fruitful.

Lord, thank you for handling me with the gentle care of a master gardener as you help me grow more fruitful.

How has God gently worked in your life?

—Beth

83. AN UNUSUAL COUSIN REUNION

Keep on loving one another as brothers and sisters.

(Hebrews 13:1)

We all remember where we were during the September 11, 2001, attacks on our country. Our young daughters had just hopped on the school bus, and I had returned to the house to watch the morning news on the television. Terry was in Istanbul, Turkey, at the Middle Eastern Soybean Conference and trade mission--hosted by the United Soybean, Indiana Soybean, and Kentucky Soybean Boards.

When broadcast anchor Tom Brokaw broke into the newscast and showed the first airplane hitting the first World Trade Center tower, I cried and immediately thought of Terry so far away. I tried to call him but couldn't get through. The next day, I received a call from him at one in the morning, telling me he and his group were safe. Terry had learned of the attacks from one of his colleagues at the conference.

Traveling abroad can always be an adventure. Sleeping in unfamiliar places, sampling exotic cuisine, and visiting area landmarks highlight the experiences. How about meeting a long-lost cousin?

Terry shared a breakfast table with USB member

Chris Davis from Minnesota during the conference. Chris noticed Terry's name badge listing Terre Haute, Indiana, as his home.

"Terry, do you know where Lewis is? My grandfather was from there."

"What was your grandfather's name?" Terry asked.

"His name was Joe."

"Did he have two brothers, Duke and Clarence, and a sister named Thelma?"

"How did you know that?"

"Because I'm Thelma's grandson."

Was it a coincidence they both ended up serving in leadership positions in the soybean industry and met each other for the first time on the other side of the globe?

Wasn't that just like God to orchestrate a faraway meeting of someone from home amid a tragedy? To foster a familial link where a once-in-a-lifetime memory was forged?

Lord, I can't help but think you smiled when those two men met. Thank you for your kind and gentle hand leading that connection.

Is there a family member you want to meet or reconnect with? Take the initiative to make that happen.

—Susan

84. LONG DISTANCE COW HERDING

> The Lord is my shepherd, I lack nothing. He makes me lie down in green pastures, he leads me beside quiet waters, he refreshes my soul. He guides me along the right paths for his name's sake.
>
> (Psalm 23:1–3)

One late summer evening, our beagle, Max, ran along the edge of our yard, howling ferociously.

"Max, what is it? What's out there, pup?"

In the dark, I couldn't see anything worth all the commotion. But when a car passed by, its headlights illuminated the light coloring of the British White cows on the other side of the road. Our neighbor had moved them to a new pasture sometime during the day. Max was adamant they were not where they belonged. His constant barking let us know all was not as it should be. But the cows weren't fazed at all. Instead, they stood silently, munching away while the crazy dog ran back and forth, howling.

God sometimes must round us up and herd us to a new location. I'm thankful he doesn't stand on the other side of the road and bark his instructions like Max. Instead, he gently guides us to a new green pasture.

Many times, the snapping voice we hear prodding us

isn't God's voice at all. Instead, someone may want us to do what they want done. The voice could be lies we've believed so long they've taken up residence in our minds. Perhaps culture is pushing us to conform. But God's voice is gentle and calm, leading us exactly where we need to go.

Lord, thank you for being the master herdsman, the gentle shepherd. Help me listen to your voice and not those standing nearby, trying to confuse me. Help me to rest, knowing I'm following your lead and under your protection.

Whose voice are you following today?

—Beth

85. MENTORING A ROOKIE

> Guide me in your truth and teach me, for you are God my Savior, and my hope is in you all day long.
>
> (Psalm 25:5)

Boy, did I need help. I was a rookie farmwife—a city girl who married a farm boy. I quickly realized Terry worked long hours and came home exhausted. I was lonely. We lived several miles from the farm, and I didn't understand this demanding new life. Who could I turn to with my questions and for understanding?

I reflected on how God had blessed me with mentors through other transitions in my life. Professionally, I had wise advisers who were respected in their professions. When raising our young daughters, I turned to Sheila, a leader in my Mothers of Preschoolers group. She advised me on how to lovingly parent two very different daughters. My first faith encourager was my neighbor, Joyce. She radiated the joy of the Lord and was a stay-at-home mom. I invited her to my high school's Ideal Woman banquet.

I determined to find a kindred spirit to serve as my farmwife mentor. The Lord directed me to Anne, one of our landlords. She'd been a farm wife for decades, had a strong faith, and was an avid listener.

Anne happily responded to any question or dilemma I presented to her. She was ready with a hug when I knocked at her back door unannounced. She kept tissues handy and reminded me marriage and farming were lifelong commitments.

Anne told me farmers have an undisputable and impenetrable connection to nature. She also said stewards of the land must learn how to balance that dedication with committed family time.

How do you find a mentor? Pray for the Lord to reveal this individual to you, then ask them if they'd like to get together for coffee or lunch and talk about your intentions.

Father God, you are our Great Encourager. Help us to be your encouragers. In your name, we pray, amen.

Ask God how he can use you to mentor others. Then follow the Lord's leading and be blessed.

—Susan

SELF-CONTROL

But the fruit of the Spirit is love, joy, peace, forbearance, kindness, goodness, faithfulness, gentleness and self-control. Against such things there is no law.

—Galatians 5:22–23

86. A RAT AND WHITE TENNIS SHOES

> May these words of my mouth and this meditation of my heart be pleasing in your sight, LORD, my Rock and my Redeemer.
>
> (Psalm 19:14)

Being a farmer's wife taught me many things. Growing up in suburbia, I never thought I would come close to meeting a rat. But, now that I have, I know two things about them: they are dumber than a box of rocks and are afraid of screaming.

Early in our marriage, we leased a hog facility. One fall after our Thanksgiving meal, Terry asked if I would like to check the pigs with him. My head said, "Are you kidding?" but my trying-to-be-an-enthusiastic-wife said, "Sure!"

When we entered the barn aisle, I stayed near the door while Terry checked the pigs. Suddenly, I looked up to see a fat rat poke its head through a hole in the wall, then run toward me.

Instinct kicked in. I screamed and jumped up and down. The rat kept coming and ran over my white tennis shoes. (Yes, I know, white shoes are not the best choice of footwear for a hog barn). He smacked into the door, turned around, and ran back over my feet and out the hole.

Where was Terry? He was laughing so hard at the

drama that he had fallen on his behind in the aisle.

I headed immediately for the truck, making him promise never to speak of this to anyone again. Unfortunately, that promise didn't hold very long.

During more than three decades of marriage, I've had countless life-on-the-farm experiences. Have I always responded calmly, appraising the situation before reacting? No. Or have I responded out of fear, frustration, or ignorance? Yes, too many times to count.

Thank goodness for God's grace and his Word. His grace indeed covers a multitude of sins. Paul minces no words in Romans 5:20–21: "The law was brought in so that the trespass might increase. But where sin increased, grace increased all the more, so that, just as sin reigned in death, so also grace might reign through righteousness to bring eternal life through Jesus Christ our Lord."

Please, Lord, keep harnessing my actions and words to better reflect you in my life.

Meditating on the Lord's Word brings peace and clarity. Spend time today with a favorite Scripture.

—Susan

87. SUNDAY MORNING CHORES

> When I was a child, I talked like a child, I thought like a child, I reasoned like a child. When I became a man, I put the ways of childhood behind me.
>
> (1 Corinthians 13:11)

When Jeff and his brother Joe were young, Sunday mornings were rushed. Their dad left them to do the farm chores while he drove to town early to host a radio show, *The Sunshine House*. Usually, the boys ran late getting done before time to leave for church. They hurried to finish, fussing with each other, and irritating their harried mom.

One Sunday, as Jeff drove the tractor back to the barn, Joe perched next to him, an idea formed in his adolescent mind. Not a good idea, but one that would ensure he got to the house before Joe.

"I'm first in the shower," Jeff shouted as he jumped from the driver's seat and ran toward the back door.

The tractor continued moving, with Joe staring in disbelief. But Jeff was confident that his younger brother would not let the tractor crash. Sure enough, conscientious Joe hopped into the driver's seat and guided the tractor safely into the shed, allowing Jeff the head start he needed.

When we are young, our decisions aren't always sound or wise. Now that Jeff is an adult, he would never jump off a running tractor. His choices today are based on the knowledge and wisdom of age and experience. No longer does he make the reckless decisions of a child.

Just as we mature physically and mentally, we need to grow spiritually. With spiritual maturity, we make wise decisions and live a spirit-filled life.

Lord, when we are tempted to run off after our desires, help us slow down and make wise decisions.

Ask God for wisdom and self-control when making decisions today.

—Beth

88. A SHORT CUT AT A FARM SHOW

The end of a matter is better than its beginning, and patience is better than pride.

(Ecclesiastes 7:8)

How many men in a minivan does it take to find the Farm Progress Show site? Does your inquiring mind want to know?

Terry, his cousins Larry and Jeff, and friend Ervin once found driving to the show in Decatur, Illinois, to be humbling but entertaining. Jeff was the designated driver while the others attempted to navigate the directions verbally.

As the group neared the show, they realized they had missed a directional sign and drove past their turn. Trying to make up for the goof, Ervin piped up from the back seat, "Let's make a California Uey."

Without thinking twice, Jeff attempted the U-turn. As he turned the van, he saw a deep ditch. While backing up to complete the turn, Jeff saw an Illinois State Trooper pull behind him. As the other three instigators sat laughing in the van, Jeff got out to show his license and registration to the police officer.

"What do you think you're doing?" the officer said.

"Something stupid," Jeff replied.

"These roads are too busy for this kind of driving," said

the officer. "Are you going to the Farm Progress Show?"

"Yes," said Jeff.

"Okay," said the officer. "Go ahead and have a good time. But, don't do any more U-turns!"

How often do we take shortcuts? We might cut an ingredient in a cake recipe and the results render a sunken baked dessert. Making fast and cheap but low-quality repairs to a car or a house can lead to more expensive repairs later.

How does the Lord view us taking shortcuts? Is he content with us when we cut corners, do a task only halfway, or rush through our daily quiet time with him each morning?

Creator of time, please help us give our all in everything we do, especially our time devoted to you. What we do minute by minute is in worship to you. In Jesus's name, amen.

Think of one way you have taken a shortcut. Ask for forgiveness and make it right.

—Susan

89. BEES WINGS

Watch and pray so that you will not fall into temptation.
The spirit is willing, but the flesh is weak.
(Matthew 26:41)

In my first harvest season of living the farm life, I was flummoxed by all the little "wings" floating around the trucks, combine, and storage bins. I was even more confused when Jeff told me they were bees' wings.

Where were all the dead bees hiding? Who was killing them? Why? And how could we stop the murders? Think of the flowers, the trees, the planet, and the people!

What a relief when I discovered the little floating things weren't actual bees' wings but the minuscule membranes that coat corn kernels and then fly off in every direction when the combine separates the parts of the plant. Oh, how they love to float around in the air and slowly drift down to cover the fields and farm lot.

After I got over my anger at all the bee murderers, I transferred my venom to the actual bees' wings. Who doesn't hate those mini-sized nuisances? Open the car for the slightest moment, and bees' wings cover the dashboard. Pull out a load of work clothes, and there they are in the lint trap. See a farmer. Cap on head. Look closely. Bees' wings are stuck to the hatband and sweaty forehead. By the end of harvest, they blanket the ground like a reddish dusting of late summer snow.

Every harvest season meant extra dusting chores to keep the bothersome bits at bay. They were everywhere I looked, and dusting was one of my least favorite tasks.

Just as harvest means constantly cleaning bees' wings, life involves vigilantly guarding our hearts and minds against the little temptations that cloud our focus from God and his best for us.

Lord, show me any tiny temptations that may have settled into my life that I need to dust away.

Have you let temptation spread into the corners of your life?

—Beth

90. A BULL MEETS A ROCK

> When the trumpets sounded, the army shouted, and at the sound of the trumpet, when the men gave a loud shout, the wall collapsed.
>
> (Joshua 6:20)

Have you ever encountered an obstacle in life's path? Not just an easily discarded object, but a barrier to your goals.

The gates of Jericho stood as an unmovable obstacle to Joshua, but we know nothing is impossible with the Lord. He had a teachable moment in store.

Joshua 6:1–3 says:

> Now the gates of Jericho were securely barred because of the Israelites. No one went out and no one came in. Then the LORD said to Joshua, 'See, I have delivered Jericho into your hands, along with its king and its fighting men. March around the city once with all the armed men. Do this for six days.' There was to be no shouting or talking, just the priests walking in front of the Ark of the Lord's Covenant continually blowing their ram's horns. On the seventh day, the Lord gave the Israelites the town.

Jericho's walls remind me of the recent sale of a Polled Hereford bull we made to a farmer. The bull bounded out of the livestock trailer into the pasture upon arriving at its new home. Getting accustomed to his spacious digs, he paced the fence line, bellowed at the farm dog, and sniffed the air for any waiting females. Suddenly, he spied a large boulder and charged for the massive rock—prancing and pawing until he came to a thundering halt. The rock didn't move. After running around several more times, the bull was convinced it was unmovable.

I remember the Lord giving me a job that promised money and notoriety. The glitz and glamour enticed me but didn't fulfill me because the Lord wasn't my priority. He allowed me to be fired so my walls of pride would crumble, and I'd depend on him.

Father Lord, we face difficulties daily. Thank you for leading us around or through them so we might grow closer to you. Amen.

What obstacle stands in front of you? Are you waiting for it to crumble? Seek the Lord with all your heart and trust him for the answer.

—Susan

91. DOWN IN A DITCH

Let your eyes look straight ahead; fix your gaze directly before you. Give careful thought to the paths for your feet and be steadfast in all your ways. Do not turn to the right or the left; keep your foot from evil.

(Proverbs 4:25–27).

"Dad, Joe's in the ditch." Words no father wants to hear.

Joe had been right behind Larry in the brown truck. But sure enough, when Larry looked out his rearview mirror, his teenage son had managed to get stuck.

Larry stopped, opened the tractor door, and motioned for Joe to join them in the cramped cab. A long, slow, miserable trip home followed.

"How?!" Larry demanded.

The tractor and truck were only going fifteen miles an hour. *How does one have a wreck at such a slow speed?* Joe had noticed a newspaper on the seat beside him. That's how.

He picked up the paper, took his eyes off the road, and began to read. Joe didn't notice the truck slowly veering to the right until he felt the bump. But he was an intelligent fellow and a decent driver for his age, so he managed to get the truck over the ditch and up into the field. Eventually, Joe would need to get back on the road.

If I can jump the ditch once, I can again.

He was wrong. Joe could get lucky only once, and the truck got stuck when he tried to jump the ditch the second time.

Younger brother Jason sat in the tractor, watching the entire escapade. He chose then to tattle. And that's how a thirty-minute errand turned into a two-hour trip involving three unhappy individuals.

How often do we do this with God? We follow him but get distracted and land in a ditch, needing him to help us out. Winding up in the wrong spot is easy when we take our eyes off God's best for us.

Lord, help us keep our eyes focused on you, following closely, veering neither to the left nor right.

Resolve to reorient your focus on God today.

—Beth

92. MASTER FARMER

> Whatever you do, work at it with all your heart, as working for the Lord, not for human masters.
> (Colossians 3:23)

According to *Indiana Prairie Farmer*, at 6 p.m. on January 31, 1928, a crowd gathered at the Fowler Hotel in Lafayette, Indiana, to honor the first nine Indiana Master Farmers. Since its inception, the program has bestowed more than three hundred awards to men and women Master Farmers or Honorary Master Farmers. Other states have followed suit with similar programs.

What is a Master Farmer? The titled program was the brainchild of Clifford Gregory, editor of *Indiana Prairie Farmer*. According to Tom Bechman, current editor, "Individuals are good farmers who mow fence rows, monitor their crops, embrace technology, and make the most of their operations. They often have state or national leadership experience and are dedicated to community and public service, their neighbors, and their faith."

Indiana Prairie Farmer and the Purdue University College of Agriculture sponsor and coordinate the program.

While the program recognizes noteworthy individuals, the Master Farmer is the Lord who calls us to emulate him.

Genesis 1:1 sets the stage. "In the beginning God created the heavens and the earth." Man's passion for the land comes straight from being made from dust. Genesis 2:7 says, "The Lord God formed a man from the dust of the ground and breathed into his nostrils the breath of life, and the man became a living being." I like to think God was happy he made farmers because Genesis 1:31 says, "God saw all that he had made, and it was very good."

Farmers are a stalwart, astute, and tenacious group, known for their patience in a profession that tests their fortitude and endurance daily. Yet, they are dedicated to their God-given passion, set the bar for ingenuity, and serve as their colleagues' mentors.

"Remember this: Whoever sows sparingly will also reap sparingly, and whoever sows generously will also reap generously" (2 Corinthians 9:6).

Father God, you sow seeds mirroring your attributes in us daily. Thank you so much. Amen.

Are you sowing seeds of Jesus's love into those around you? The Lord has much to teach us as we farm in his name.

—Susan

93. AUGER MIRACLE

Be alert and of sober mind. Your enemy the devil prowls around like a roaring lion looking for someone to devour.

(1 Peter 5:8)

My brother-in-law, Jason, was a big, tough, high school football player. That's probably the only reason he survived his run-in with the auger. One day, Jason's job was to grind the grain to feed the animals.

A small bolt took him down. Jason moved one step too close to the powerful machine. Instantly, his overalls caught on a protruding bolt, and the augur shaft pulled him in. His pants twisted tighter and tighter. Death or a severe maiming was imminent.

Suddenly, Jason's overalls gave way, and the force flipped him up and over the drill. He landed hard on the rocky drive, bruised and dazed. Slowly, Jason stood and checked for injuries. Adrenaline rushed through his body as he wondered how he had survived the last few minutes. He headed to the house where his mom had watched in fear and disbelief. Her precious son had battled an auger and won.

Just like that little bolt that took down my giant brother-in-law, Satan tries to take us down with tiny, unexpected temptations. A few small steps away from God can expose us to unhealthy desires that pull us in, twist us up, and destroy us. But, if we are lucky, they only flip us up and knock us to the ground, leaving us bruised.

Living our lives in a close relationship with God and as far from temptation as possible is essential.

Lord, may our eyes be watchful and our minds alert to those things that pull us away from you and toward danger.

What little "bolts" do you need to watch out for in your life?

—Beth

94. PURSUING GOD-GIVEN PASSIONS

> The LORD makes firm the steps of the one who delights in him; though he may stumble, he will not fall, for the LORD upholds him with his hand.
>
> (Psalm 37:23–24)

Terry and I strove to guide our two daughters toward their God-given passions. Why? This philosophy was cemented in me early in our dating when I asked Terry why he wanted to be a farmer. He immediately responded, "I've known since I was fourteen that I wanted to study agriculture at Purdue University and return to the family farm."

He was so sure and content with that decision, even from an early age.

Terry's passion for farming mirrored my dad's love of the outdoors. Dad was an assistant professor of forestry and a Purdue wildlife extension agent for nearly thirty years, covering the state of Indiana. His job provided many opportunities to fish and hunt.

Mom's gift was hospitality. She exuded it in sales and leadership positions, reveling in every facet of making people feel welcome and pampered. My bent toward writing started in high school but blossomed when writing for the *Purdue Exponent* and the *Purdue Alumnus*. I've freelanced for thirty years.

Lillian inherited her love of cattle and farming from her dad. She has known she wanted to be involved in agriculture since she was a teenager. Now she and her husband, Kegan, farm with us. Hayley became a fashionista in her preschool years, often wearing clothes from the dress-up box when she went to the grocery store with me. Hayley joined 4-H, began sewing, and hasn't stopped. Her fashion design career is based in London.

Encouraging our girls to dream big, take specific courses, and seize experiences in their chosen interests channeled their directions while they trusted the Lord for their paths. Prayer was our life support.

Father God, you created us definitively and purposefully. Thank you for the gifts and abilities planted in each of us.

Are you following your God-given passion? It's not too late to start.

—Susan

95. TOWN DAY

She is like the merchant ships, bringing her food from afar.

(Proverbs 31:14)

Growing up in town, I'd never heard of town day. But when we moved to the farm, I soon learned the reality of living far from stores and restaurants. No more delivery pizza for me. No quick stops to pick up that forgotten gallon of milk. Forget about the possibility of an impulse stop at the Tasty Freeze, Dairy Barn, or whatever the local ice cream shop was called.

Once I'd moved to the farm, my mother-in-law, Rita, taught me that Thursday was her town day. And boy, was Thursday a full day. We did all errands, doctor's appointments, and shopping on this special day. Town Day was also a time to visit friends and family.

Once the girls boarded the school bus, we packed and headed north to town. For me, town day involved library time with the preschooler. Then lunch with friends or at the pizza/playland, followed by grocery shopping before the mid-afternoon toddler meltdown. I'd pull into the driveway moments before the bus dropped off the older girls.

I lived for town day—not just because I got to eat out but because I needed groceries by Thursday. I took a long time to learn to plan for an entire week without shopping, and even longer to learn to adapt when I ran out of items like toilet paper before town day. Thank God for family living nearby. Living outside the city meant learning self-control, making do without, being creative with what I did have, and staying organized. I didn't like the weekly habit initially, but the habits town day created became a way of life that I'm thankful to have learned.

Lord, thank you for all that this farm lifestyle teaches us.

What has living a farm life taught you?

—Beth

96. COW SIGHTINGS

> The mind governed by the flesh is death, but the mind governed by the Spirit is life and peace.
>
> (Romans 8:6)

I firmly believe God brings us laughter in trying situations.

My hands were immersed in sudsy dishwater when the phone rang. Our friend, Brent, who lived about two miles away and behind a pasture we use, was calling.

"Susan, I think one of your Polled Hereford cows is out of the pasture. I tried to turn her around for about a half mile, but she'd just run into a field. I backtracked to call you."

Oh, great. A cow was on the loose, and Terry was on his way to pick up tractor parts an hour south of us. I called him to relay the news. While he headed home, my phone rang again.

"Susan, I think one of your cows just passed our house," Nancy, another friend, reported. "The cow is traveling at a brisk clip." She lived a half mile east of the first cow sighting.

By this time, I was laughing as I called Terry again. He had summoned our farm workers to pick up the chase with the farm truck, a livestock trailer, and a "lure" cow.

When I found everyone, the big-hooved escape artist was circling the trailer and slowly meandering into it. We calculated the cow had traveled five miles of county roads and ravines. Its name? Slowpoke!

Livestock don't always go where you want them to. Isn't that just like we humans? We often go anywhere but where the Lord wants. Thank goodness for his grace, mercy, and creative ways of leading us back to him.

So many times, Lord, I procrastinate or am just plain stubborn. Thank you for your patience with us, even though you sometimes must prod us to pay attention.

Do you crave your own way? Does your desire for control make life frustrating for others? Take it to the Lord in prayer.

—Susan

97. THE SECRET MISSION

Do everything without grumbling or arguing.
(Philippians 2:14)

"Where are we going, Mommy?"

I dreaded hearing that question from my four-year-old.

"Oh, just out for a drive. We're going to take Nanny (otherwise known as Grandma). Let's eat lunch with her. How does that sound?"

"Fun!" she giggled from her car seat.

I was not about to tell her the real reason for our errand. We were picking up boar semen. I was trying not to *think* about the purpose too much myself.

We drove through the back roads to another farm specializing in the aforementioned commodity. I ran into the cement building—carefully watching each of my steps—to pick up our purchase while Nanny sat in the car with Jaena. Inside, I discreetly held my hand over my nose, unsuccessfully attempting to block out the sickening scent without drawing any attention to my dislike of the "smell of money."

Soon, I walked out with a Styrofoam container full of precious liquid and the implements needed to use said liquid. I carefully placed the box as far back in the van as possible, and we were off. Nanny, Jaena, and I found a cute country cafe and had a "lovely" lunch. I'm not sure "lovely" is the right word considering I was trying with all my might to eat, despite knowing what sat in the back of my car. Gross! Best of all, Jaena never knew the real reason for the trip.

I've learned that living on a farm means being asked to do strange and even unpleasant errands. It's best to get on with the job and make the best of it.

Lord, give us the strength to do the jobs we don't want to do. And help us not to grumble while completing them.

How can you make the best of a bad situation today?

—Beth

98. FIRST FRUITS

> Bring the best of the firstfruits of your soil to the house of the LORD your God.
>
> (Exodus 23:19)

Have you ever known someone who not only diligently tithed a tenth to their church but also espoused to live on only ten percent of their income?

This life lesson was shared with Terry and me when we visited Broetje Orchards, near Prescott, Washington, in the fall of 1999. As participants of Indiana Farm Bureau, Inc.'s Agricultural Cultural Exchange Ambassador program, we were selected to learn about Washington state's agriculture and share our observations when we returned to Indiana.

Founded by Ralph and Cheryl Broetje in 1988—with their biblically named brand, First Fruits of Washington—they built their enterprise on apple orchards and cherry acreage. Ralph, a humble and quiet man, explained that their orchard operation was one of the four largest in the world and the only ones with sole proprietorship. They were also noted for embracing vertical integration because they grew, packaged, and shipped all on one site.

What makes the Broetje's unique? The couple lives by the scriptural principles of giving their first fruits. They chose to live on ten percent of their income to provide the ninety percent to missions and charity.

Broetje's generosity and servant leadership shine through their building of two housing communities for their seasonal- and year-round employees. An early childhood center, laundromat, market, fuel station, cafe, post office, and medical clinic benefit the people who Broetje's depend upon.

Valuing his business's leadership team, Ralph built homes for them among the apple orchards that stretch nearly ten miles over breathtaking rolling ground. Establishing such housing opportunities for employees was precedent-setting in the industry.

When Ralph was fifteen, he listened to a missionary talking about children suffering in India. Even then, he dreamed of having an apple orchard to help Indian children. Ultimately, he and Cheryl adopted six children from Calcutta and Bombay, India, adding to their three biological children.

Broetje's commitment to living biblically and giving enthusiastically locally, nationally, and internationally is the cornerstone of their business and more than fifty years of marriage.

You're all about giving unselfishly, Lord. Lead my heart to beat like yours.

Spend time reflecting on how you can use your resources to help others.

—Susan

99. HAWK AT THE BIRDFEEDER

Does the hawk take flight by your wisdom and spread its wings toward the south?

(Job 39:26)

"Mom, come quick. What's that giant bird?"

I rushed to join Jessica at the kitchen window. Outside the glass stood a hawk the size of a swan but definitely not as pretty. I was instantly outraged. *Why is he so near the birdfeeder? Is he after the lovely doves that have made a nest nearby? Will he scare away all the colorful finches?* If the window had been open, I might have reached out and shooed him away—if I had the guts.

I am glad I didn't because Mr. Hawk was in my yard for a better reason than bullying tiny birds. He held a snake in his talons. This bird of prey had protected me from my great enemy, the snake, who perhaps lived in our crawl space or attempted to climb the side of our house. Eww. I hate to think about how close the snake had been to my house.

Mr. Hawk looked at me as if to say, "Aren't you gonna thank me?"

Thank you, indeed, Mr. Hawk. I smiled and watched him fly off to enjoy his treetop dinner.

Protection comes in many forms—sometimes as a hawk but at other times by loving parents or concerned friends. In an emergency, we call on firefighters and police for help. But God is the ultimate protector, watching over us with his omnipresence. He's a refuge in troubling times and a shield when arrows fly.

Lord, thank you for watching over and protecting us in times of need. Thank you for helping us when we aren't even aware we need help.

Name a way God has been faithful in protecting you.

—Beth

100. A LESSON FROM A WOODPECKER

> And God said, 'Let the water teem with living creatures, and let birds fly above the earth across the vault of the sky.'
>
> (Genesis 1:20)

Rat-a-tat-tat. Rat-a-tat-tat. What was that incessant noise so early in the morning? Walking on our farm road, I basked in the newness of the day when this unwelcome racket interrupted me. Slowing to search out the location of the ruckus, I suddenly spied him—a pileated woodpecker.

If my late dad had been with me, he would have immediately adjusted his ever-present binoculars hanging around his neck and taken in the bird's beauty rather than complain about its drumming.

Dad would have quietly noted the bird's love of deciduous or mixed forests and its markedly crested plumages, with a noteworthy scarlet red topknot. The woodpecker's drumming is distinctive and loud, yet progressively softer at the end.

To human observation, the bird banged his head and heart out to create tiny holes in a hard tree. To what end? Probably in search of tasty bugs. Why did God make the bird so hard-headed? To be resilient, strong, and tenacious at their task.

Should the Lord expect anything less of us? Of course not. He expects more.

Paul wrote, "Whatever you do, work at it with all your heart, as working for the Lord, not for human masters" (Colossians 3:23).

As God gave us dominion over the earth—including the birds of the air—the Holy Spirit fills us with the resolve to accomplish the daily and future tasks he gives us to honor him. If a small bird can pound out a day's work with flair and dedication, I can do much more through Christ, who gives me strength.

Lord, you do have a purpose for being hard-headed. Help me to be resilient and resolute in accomplishing what you've given me to do.

Do you have a deadline, a project to prepare, or a meeting to lead? Remember the pileated woodpecker who seizes his work with unyielding strength and perseverance.

—Susan

ABOUT THE AUTHORS

Beth Gormong has coauthored two women's devotional books with Jeanette Levellie: *Hello, Beautiful!* and *Yes, You Can!* Beth has contributed to *Evenings with Jesus*, a *Guideposts* book, as well as regularly writing in *Guideposts* magazine, *Strength & Grace Daily Devotions*, and other publications. Like Susan, she is a city girl who married a farmer and lived in a century-old farmhouse surrounded by fields and hogs for twenty-eight years. In 2022, Beth's husband, Jeff, retired from farming, and the empty nesters moved to the city. In addition to writing, Beth works as the Administrative Assistant to the Director of Publishing at Wesleyan Publishing House, runs the Green Gable Studio Etsy shop, reads the Bible from front to back every year, and loves encouraging others in their walk with Jesus. Follow Beth at bgormong.com.

Susan Hayhurst is a farmwife work in progress. Marrying her farmer husband, Terry, nearly thirty-five years ago, challenged her—a city girl—to bloom where she was planted. Susan has written for tourism, economic development, and agricultural magazines and publications for thirty years. Her fresh and quirky perspective about living on an active grain and livestock farm produces endless inspiration for her "Hayhurst's Hayloft" humor columns in *Indiana Prairie Farmer* magazine, garnering her a loyal readership. She served as a leader for Moms in Prayer while her girls were growing up. She is a board member for Youth for Christ of the Wabash Valley and strives always to be a prayer warrior. Susan and Terry live on a farm in southwestern Indiana. When she's not accidentally sitting on electric fences or popping wheelies with a tractor, Susan indulges in writing, reading, pining for a Florida beach, and doting on her two granddaughters. Follow Susan at susanhayhurst.com.

Made in the USA
Columbia, SC
19 February 2023